Ordnance Survey
Wye Valley and Forest of Dean
Walks

Pathfinder Guide
Compiled by Brian Conduit

JARROLD

D0486992

Key to colour coding

The walks are divided into three broad categories, indicated by the following colours:

Short, easy walks

Walks of moderate length, likely to involve some modest uphill walking

More challenging walks, which may be longer and/or over more rugged terrain, often with some stiff climbs

Acknowledgements

I am grateful to the following for their advice and assistance: Mr P. W. Ralph (Forestry Commission), Mr N. R. Hayes (Gloucestershire County Council), Mr L. Chambers (Hereford and Worcester County Council) and Mr G. Probert (Gwent County Council).

While every care has been taken to ensure the accuracy of the route directions, the publishers cannot accept responsibility for errors or omissions, or for changes in details given. It has to be emphasised that the countryside is not static: hedges and fences can be removed, field boundaries can alter, footpaths can be rerouted and changes of ownership can result in the closure or diversion of some concessionary paths. Also paths that are easy and pleasant for walking in fine conditions may become slippery, muddy and difficult in wet weather and stepping stones over rivers and streams may become impassable. If readers know of any changes which have taken place, or have noticed any inaccuracies, Jarrold Publishing would be grateful to hear from them.

Ordnance Survey   ISBN 0-319-00246-2
Jarrold Publishing   ISBN 0-7117-0549-6

First published 1991 by Ordnance Survey and Jarrold Publishing

Ordnance Survey   Jarrold Publishing
Romsey Road   Barrack Street
Maybush   Norwich NR3 1TR
Southampton SO9 4DH

© Crown copyright 1991

Printed in Great Britain by Jarrold Printing, Norwich. 1/91

Previous page: *Tintern Abbey, with the wooded slopes of the Forest of Dean beyond*

Contents

Walks

Introduction to the Wye Valley and Forest of Dean

The Wye is a long river. Like its neighbour the Severn it rises on the slopes of Plynlimmon and eventually disgorges into the Severn estuary just below Chepstow. Unlike the Severn it is as much a Welsh river (Afon Gwy) as an English one. Its journey from source to sea falls naturally into three sections: initially it flows south-eastwards through mid-Wales, then it enters England to curve eastwards and southwards through Herefordshire, and finally it heads south-wards through a spectacular limestone gorge. In this last section it serves as the well-defined border between the two countries.

To the east of this gorge in the lower Wye Valley rise the densely wooded slopes of the Forest of Dean, occupying a roughly triangular-shaped plateau which separates the Wye from the Severn. The eastern flanks of the forest look down on the broad sweep of the Severn and across the Vale of Gloucester to the Cotswold escarpment; the views from its western edge have the distant Black Mountains on the horizon. To the south the forest reaches almost to the meeting of the two rivers at the apex of the triangle, and from its northern edge there are views across the farmlands of Herefordshire to the Malverns. For much of its history the forest has been a strangely secretive and 'cut off' part of the country and even today, despite the proximity of motorways and influx of tourists, this 'land between two rivers' still retains something of that inward-looking and remote feel.

In some ways the Wye Valley and the Forest of Dean are two quite different and separate regions, though they are indissolubly linked by geology, geography and history. Geologically both areas are underlain by carboniferous rocks, a mixture of coal measures, conglomerates, limestones and chiefly red sandstones. Geographically they are neighbours, the forest forming the eastern rim of the valley for much of the Wye's lower reaches. Historically both valley and forest share a common heritage as a border area between England and Wales. Apart from the gorge between Monmouth and Chepstow, the Wye Valley is broad and open, almost entirely rural and unspoilt, its typically English landscape punctuated by a series of some of the most attractive old market towns and appealing villages as could be found anywhere. In contrast the Forest of Dean is an enclosed world of thick woodland, with few pre-Victorian towns and villages and with a long industrial tradition, although the last twenty to thirty years have erased most traces of the latter.

This walking guide focuses on the middle and lower sections of the Wye Valley, roughly where the river leaves its upper reaches in mid-Wales to enter Herefordshire. Hay-on-Wye and Hereford are thus the approximate northern limits. The other boundaries are more obvious: the River Severn to the east, the Bristol Channel to the south and the eastern wall of the Black Mountains forming a well-defined boundary on the west.

The Wye Valley

A discerning traveller following the course of the River Wye will soon be aware of the major historic theme running through the region — the frontier. This is England's western borderland, the country of the Welsh Marches, and both sides of the river are littered with the ruins of often imposing and substantial medieval castles.

Some of the prominent higher points were utilised for much earlier defences. Both Dinedor Hill overlooking Hereford and Capler Hill which commands a particularly spectacular viewpoint above the river are crowned by the earthworks of Iron Age defences. To the Romans the Wye was the approximate limit of their civil zone; westwards lay the military zone peopled by the warlike Silures of South Wales. After the departure of the Romans, in the Dark Ages the native Britons or Welsh struggled to stem the advancing tide of Anglo-Saxon conquest. Again the Wye Valley was the most westerly limit of that conquest, evidenced by the remarkable dyke, constructed by the Mercian king Offa the Great (757 – 796), that runs for nearly 150 miles (240 km), from the Dee estuary in the north to the Severn estuary in the south, clearly defining the border between Mercia and the territories of the Welsh princes, the border between Anglo-Saxon and Celt. Whether Offa's Dyke was purely a frontier or had a military function as well remains a source of historical controversy, but if it was supposed to act as a defence it was not very effective, as the following centuries saw much warfare between English and Welsh.

It was the Norman conquerors who began the systematic penetration across the border into Wales. William the Conqueror granted lands and special privileges to the Marcher Lords in return for their guarding the borderlands. In the 'southern marches' of the Wye Valley the most powerful of these lords was William Fitz Osbern, Earl of Hereford, who built the first great castles at Chepstow,

View over the Wye Valley from Capler Lodge

Monmouth and Hereford, beginning a sequence of castle building; Goodrich, St Briavels and Raglan followed in the twelfth century and, as the Marcher Lords thrust forward into Gwent, the 'Trilateral' castles of the Monnow valley (White Castle, Grosmont and Skenfrith) were built in the thirteenth century.

These castles are the most striking reminder of the centuries of warfare along the English-Welsh border. Less obvious are the border churches, many with fortress-like towers, that ordinary people used as places of refuge during raids. Two of the finest of these are situated within a short distance of each other in the Monnow valley: at Skenfrith by the banks of the river on the Welsh side of the border, and at Garway high up above the valley on the English side. Ecclesiastical buildings of a less warlike appearance are the magnificent remains of the three great monastic foundations at Tintern, Llanthony and Abbey Dore.

Edward I's conquest of Wales in the later thirteenth century brought more security to the border, and with greater security came greater prosperity and the development of agriculture. The rich, red earth enabled Herefordshire to develop into a major arable and fruit-growing area. Red is the predominant colour of the Wye Valley, with the red earth of the ploughed fields and the red sandstone of the church towers at Mordiford, King's Caple, Sellack, Ross-on-Wye and, finest of all, Hereford Cathedral.

Towards the end of the eighteenth century the Wye Valley, especially the gorge area of the lower Wye, was discovered by the Romantics, intellectual and aristocratic visitors who found the combination of steep, wooded cliffs, winding river and the spectacular viewpoints of Wintour's Leap, Wynd Cliff, Devil's Pulpit and above all Symonds Yat irresistibly 'wild' and 'picturesque', especially when the scene was further enhanced by equally striking man-made features like the ruins of Goodrich Castle and Tintern Abbey. Wordsworth was one of those impressed by the beauty of the region and composed some of his most memorable lines in the vicinity of Tintern Abbey.

The Romantics who came here to do the 'Wye Tour', travelling leisurely by boat down the river from Ross-on-Wye to Chepstow, were the precursors of the later tourists who have flocked here — using different and less relaxing modes of transport but attracted by the same scenic and historic features.

The Forest of Dean

The Forest of Dean's landscape has been moulded by the variety of roles that the forest has served throughout its history: industrial region, royal hunting ground, supplier of timber and latterly recreational and tourist area.

The industrial role is the longest lasting, stretching back to the Romans who began the mining of coal and iron in the region. This continued over the centuries and quarrying and iron-smelting followed. Industrial activity reached its peak during the second half of the nineteenth century and in the years just before the First World War. At the time iron production was at its greatest, coal-mining was flourishing (some of the mines had extremely colourful names such as 'Go On and Prosper' and 'Strip and At It'), a maze of railway lines ran through the forest and many of the villages and towns had expanded, especially Coleford, Cinderford and Lydney.

After the First World War the story was one of decline, considerably accelerated after the Second World War. The railways closed down, iron-mining ended and coal production virtually ceased — the last major pit closed in 1965 — apart from the handful of small 'tree mines', operated by independent miners who maintain a tradition said to go back to the thirteenth century. Now the traces, or some might say scars, of these industries have almost disappeared as a result of the demolition of redundant buildings, planting of conifers and landscaping of derelict sites.

After the Romans exploited the forest for its mineral resources, Norman kings exploited it for its sport. William the Conqueror made it a royal forest, a private hunting-ground for himself and his successors, with its own code of laws and forest courts. Headquarters of the forest administration was St Briavels Castle, the Constable of the Castle also being Warden of the Forest, responsible for enforcing the forest laws that were designed both to protect the royal game, mainly deer and boar, and preserve the trees and undergrowth that sheltered them. The royal forests reached their greatest extent in the thirteenth century, when collectively they covered nearly a third of the country, but then decline set in. Later monarchs were more interested in them as commercial assets rather than playgrounds and consequently trees were felled, clearances made, land was sold off and the forest laws lapsed and became largely obsolete.

The Forest of Dean fared somewhat differently from most of the other royal forests, hence its more complete survival. Many of the woodlands were felled as its timber was much in demand, both as a source of charcoal for the local iron-smelting industries and as building material for the navy. Indeed its fame as a supplier of good quality timber for warships must have spread far and wide as it is said that the commanders of the Spanish Armada were ordered to 'be sure not to leave a tree standing in the Forest of Dean'. But after many vicissitudes, much destruction and several changes of ownership in the political turmoil of the Civil War and Cromwellian period, the Crown ultimately retained ownership and in the reign of Charles II inaugurated a series of enclosures for the purposes of preserving and replanting. At the same time the Speech House was built as a new headquarters for the revitalised forest, and although it is now a hotel it is still used for meetings of the Forest Courts.

Towards the end of the eighteenth century the first conifers appeared and in the early nineteenth century large-scale plantations of both conifers and oaks were ordered by the Admiralty to replenish the deficiencies in timber resources revealed by the Napoleonic Wars. Ironically before these had matured they were no longer needed for the purpose of building naval vessels — iron steamships had replaced the wooden warships of Nelson's time — but these plantations are responsible for some of the finest oak woodlands in the forest today.

The First World War depleted Britain's timber resources even more rapidly and consequently the Forestry Commission was set up in 1919 to remedy this. A few years later the Forest of Dean came under its control and a large programme of establishing conifer plantations commenced. But the Commission was also aware of the recreational as well as the commercial value of the forest, and has conserved its ancient woodlands and tried to preserve its traditional nature and appearance by maintaining a judicious balance between conifers and broad-leaved trees. In 1938 the Forest of Dean became a National Forest Park and since the end of the Second World War the Forestry Commission has emphasised and developed its amenities as a tourist and recreational area by the provision of car parks, picnic sites and waymarked trails.

What was once the private playground of kings is now a public playground where all can enjoy wandering along quiet, secluded tracks through some of the most beautiful and extensive woodlands in the country.

Walking in the area
With a tremendous variety of scenery, wealth of historic attractions and selection of waymarked paths, the Wye Valley and the Forest of Dean together make excellent walking country. The scenic delights embrace the bare moorlands on the eastern edge of the Black Mountains, the rolling country of the Wye and Golden valleys, the dense woodlands of the Forest of Dean, the dramatic limestone gorge of the lower Wye and the gentle landscapes around Dymock and Newent. Historic attractions include monastic remains, the ruins of the great border castles and relics of the region's industrial heritage, as well as the pleasant old market towns and interesting villages.

The well-waymarked paths that thread their way through the area make for generally trouble-free route finding; the best known of these are Offa's Dyke Path and the Wye Valley Walk. Many public footpaths in the Forest of Dean are waymarked as well as the Forestry Commission trails. Away from these popular routes some of the paths are more difficult to follow, especially in the Monnow and Golden Valley regions of western Herefordshire, where rights of way have become obliterated through lack of use and

Ruardean and the Wye Valley from Ruardean Hill, on the northern edge of the Forest of Dean

maintenance. Here some of the relatively traffic-free country lanes are often a better proposition.

The following selection of walks makes full use of all these assets, enabling you to sample the many and varied delights of this beautiful and historic region.

The National Trust

Anyone who likes visiting places of natural beauty and/or historic interest has cause to be grateful to the National Trust. Without it, many such places would probably have vanished by now, either under an avalanche of concrete and bricks and mortar or through reservoir construction or blanket afforestation.

It was in response to the pressures on the countryside posed by the relentless march of Victorian industrialisation that the Trust was set up in 1895. Its founders, inspired by the common goals of protecting and conserving Britain's national heritage and widening public access to it, were Sir Robert Hunter, Octavia Hill and Canon Rawnsley; a solicitor, a social reformer and a clergyman respectively. The latter was particularly influential. As a canon of Carlisle Cathedral and vicar of Crosthwaite (near Keswick), he was concerned about threats to the Lake District and had already been active in protecting footpaths and promoting public access to open countryside. After the flooding of Thirlmere in 1879 to create a large reservoir, he and his two colleagues became increasingly convinced that the only effective protection was outright ownership of land.

The purpose of the National Trust is to preserve areas of natural beauty and sites of historic interest by acquisition, holding them in trust for the nation and making them available for public access and enjoyment. Some of its properties have been acquired through purchase, but many have been donated. Nowadays it is not only one of the biggest landowners in the country, but also one of the most active conservation charities, protecting well over half a million acres of land, including over 500 miles of coastline and a large number of historic properties (houses, castles and gardens) in England, Wales and Northern Ireland. (There is a separate National Trust for Scotland, which was set up in 1931.)

Furthermore, once a piece of land has come under Trust ownership, it is difficult for its status to be altered. As a result of Parliamentary legislation in 1907, the Trust was given the right to declare its property inalienable, so ensuring that in any dispute it can appeal directly to Parliament.

As it works towards its dual aims of conserving areas of attractive countryside and encouraging greater public access (not easy to reconcile in this age of mass tourism), the Trust provides an excellent service to walkers by creating new concessionary paths and waymarked trails, by maintaining stiles and footbridges and by combating the ever-increasing problem of footpath erosion.

For details of membership, contact the National Trust at the address on page 78.

The Ramblers' Association

No organisation works more actively to protect and extend the rights and interests of walkers in the countryside than the Ramblers' Association. Its aims (summarised here) are clear: to foster a greater knowledge, love and care of the countryside; to assist in the protection and enhancement of public rights of way and areas of natural beauty; to work for greater public access to the countryside and to encourage more people to take up rambling as a healthy, recreational activity.

It was founded in 1935 when, following the setting up of a National Council of Ramblers' Federation in 1931, a number of federations earlier formed in London, Manchester, the Midlands and elsewhere came together to create a more effective pressure group, to deal with such contemporary problems as the disappearance and obstruction of footpaths, the prevention of access to open mountain and moorland and increasing hostility from landowners. This was the era of the mass trespasses, when there were sometimes violent confrontations between ramblers and gamekeepers, especially on the moorlands of the Peak District.

Since then the Ramblers' Association has played an influential role in preserving and developing the national footpath network, supporting the creation of National Parks and

The Wye from Huntsham Bridge

bridleways are shown by broken green lines on Ordnance Survey Pathfinder and Outdoor Leisure maps and broken red lines on Landranger maps. There is also a third category, called byways or 'roads used as a public path': chiefly broad, walled tracks (green lanes) or farm roads, which walkers, riders and cyclists have to share, usually only occasionally, with motor vehicles. Many of these public paths have been in existence for hundreds of years and some even originated as prehistoric trackways and have been in constant use for well over 2,000 years.

The term 'right of way' means exactly what it says. It gives right of passage over what, in the vast majority of cases, is private land, and you are required to keep to the line of the path and not stray onto the land either side. If you inadvertently wander off the right of way — either because of faulty map-reading or because the route is not clearly indicated on the ground — you are technically trespassing and the wisest course is to ask the nearest available person (farmer or fellow walker) to direct you back to the correct route. There are stories of unpleasant confrontations between walkers and farmers at times, but in general most farmers are helpful and co-operative when responding to a genuine and polite request for assistance in route finding.

Obstructions can sometimes be a problem and probably the commonest of these is where a path across a field has been ploughed up. It is legal for a farmer to plough up a path provided that he restores it within two weeks, barring exceptionally bad weather. This does not always happen and here the walker is presented with a dilemma. Does he follow the line of the path, even if this inevitably means treading on crops, or does he use his common sense and walk around the edge of the field? The latter course of action often seems the best but, as this means that you would be trespassing, you are, in law, supposed to keep to the exact line of the path, avoiding unnecessary damage to crops. In the case of other obstructions which may block a path (illegal fences and locked gates etc.), common sense again has to be used in order to negotiate them by the easiest method (detour or removal). If you have any problems negotiating rights of way, you should report the matter to the Rights of Way Department of the relevant county, borough or metropolitan district council. They will then take action with the landowner concerned.

Apart from rights of way enshrined by law, there are a number of other paths available to walkers. Permissive or concessionary paths have been created where a landowner has given permission for the public to use a particular route across his land. The main problem with these is that, as they have been

encouraging the designation and way-marking of long-distance footpaths.

Our freedom to walk in the countryside is precarious, and requires constant vigilance. As well as the perennial problems of footpaths being illegally obstructed, disappearing through lack of use or extinguished by housing or road construction, new dangers can spring up at any time.

It is to meet such problems and dangers that the Ramblers' Association exists and represents the interests of all walkers. The address to write to for information on the Ramblers' Association and how to become a member is given on page 78.

Walkers and the law

The average walker in a National Park or other popular walking area, armed with the appropriate Ordnance Survey map, reinforced perhaps by a guidebook giving detailed walking instructions, is unlikely to run into legal difficulties, but it is useful to know something about the law relating to public rights of way. The right to walk over certain parts of the countryside has developed over a long period of time, and how such rights came into being and how far they are protected by the law is a complex subject, fascinating in its own right, but too lengthy to be discussed here. The following comments are intended simply to be a helpful guide, backed up by the Countryside Access Charter, a concise summary of walkers' rights and obligations drawn up by the Countryside Commission.

Basically there are two main kinds of public rights of way: footpaths (for walkers only) and bridleways (for walkers, riders on horseback and pedal cyclists). Footpaths and granted as a concession, there is no legal right to use them and therefore they can be extinguished at any time. In practice, many of these concessionary routes have been established on land owned either by large public bodies such as the Forestry Commission, or by a private one, such as the National Trust, and as these mainly encourage walkers to use their paths, they are unlikely to be closed unless a change of ownership occurs.

Walkers also have free access to Country Parks (except where requested to keep away from certain areas for ecological reasons, e.g. wildlife protection, woodland re-generation, safeguarding of rare plants etc.), canal towpaths and most beaches. By custom, though not by right, you are generally free to walk across the open and uncultivated higher land of mountain, moor-land and fell, but this varies from area to area and from one season to another — grouse moors, for example, will be out of bounds during the breeding and shooting seasons and some open areas are used as Ministry of Defence firing ranges, for which reason access will be restricted. In some areas the situation has been clarified as a result of 'access agreements' between the landowners and either the county council or the National Park authority, which clearly define when and where you can walk over such open country.

Countryside Access Charter

Your rights of way are:
- Public footpaths — on foot only. Sometimes waymarked in yellow
- Bridleways — on foot, horseback and pedal cycle. Sometimes waymarked in blue
- Byways (usually old roads), most 'roads used as public paths' and, of course, public roads — all traffic has the right of way

Use maps, signs and waymarks to check rights of way. Ordnance Survey Pathfinder and Landranger maps show most public rights of way

On rights of way you can:
- take a pram, pushchair or wheelchair if practicable
- take a dog (on a lead or under close control)
- take a short route round an illegal obstruction or remove it sufficiently to get past

You have a right to go for recreation to:
- public parks and open spaces — on foot
- most commons near older towns and cities — on foot and sometimes on horseback
- private land where the owner has a formal agreement with the local authority

In addition you can use the following by local or established custom or consent, but ask for advice if you are unsure:
- many areas of open country, such as moorland, fell and coastal areas, especially those in the care of the National Trust, and some commons
- some woods and forests, especially those owned by the Forestry Commission
- Country Parks and picnic sites
- most beaches
- canal towpaths
- some private paths and tracks

Consent sometimes extends to horse-riding and cycling

For your information:
- county councils and London boroughs maintain and record rights of way, and register commons
- obstructions, dangerous animals, harassment and misleading signs on rights of way are illegal and you should report them to the county council
- paths across fields can be ploughed, but must normally be reinstated within two weeks
- landowners can require you to leave land to which you have no right of access
- motor vehicles are normally permitted only on roads, byways and some 'roads used as public paths'

Stately beeches crown the summit of Dinedor Hill

Key Map

SCALE 1:250 000 or 4 MILES to 1 INCH

0 1 km   0·6214 mile 5   10   Kilometres 15

0 1 mile   1·61 kms   5   Miles   10

CONVENTIONAL SIGNS 1:25 000 or 2½ INCHES to 1 MILE

ROADS AND PATHS

Not necessarily rights of way

M 1 or A 6(M)	M 1 or A 6(M)	Motorway
A 31 (T)	A 31 (T)	Trunk road
A 35	A 35	Main road
B 3074	B 3074	Secondary road
A 35	A 35	Dual carriageway

Narrow roads with passing places are annotated

Road generally more than 4m wide

Road generally less than 4m wide

Other road, drive or track

Unfenced roads and tracks are shown by pecked lines

.... Path

RAILWAYS

Multiple track ⎫
Single track ⎬ Standard gauge

Narrow gauge

Siding

Cutting

Embankment

Tunnel

Road over & under

Level crossing; station

PUBLIC RIGHTS OF WAY   Public rights of way may not be evident on the ground

- - - - - - - ⎫ Public paths ⎧ Footpath
————— ⎭ ⎩ Bridleway

+ + + + + Byway open to all traffic
⊥ ⊥ ⊥ ⊥ Road used as a public path

DANGER AREA
Firing and test ranges in the area
Danger!
Observe warning notices

The indication of a towpath in this book does not necessarily imply a public right of way
The representation of any other road, track or path is no evidence of the existence of a right of way

BOUNDARIES

— · — · — · — County (England and Wales)

— — — — — District

⊶⊶⊶⊶⊶ London Borough

· · · · · · · · · · · · · · Civil Parish (England)* Community (Wales)

— — — — — — Constituency (County, Borough, Burgh or European Assembly)

⎫ Coincident boundaries are shown by
⎬ the first appropriate symbol
⎭
*For Ordnance Survey purposes County
Boundary is deemed to be the limit of the
parish structure whether or not a parish
area adjoins

SYMBOLS

⚑	Place	with tower	
⚐	of	with spire, minaret or dome	
+	worship	without such additions	

⊞ △ Glasshouse; youth hostel

⊷ Bus or coach station

⚓ ⚓ ⚓ Lighthouse; lightship; beacon

△ Triangulation station

Triangulation point on ⎧ church or chapel
⎨ lighthouse, beacon
⎩ building; chimney

pylon pole Electricity transmission line

VILLA Roman antiquity (AD 43 to AD 420)

Castle Other antiquities

⊹ Site of antiquity

⚔ 1066 Site of battle (with date)

Gravel pit

Sand pit

Chalk pit, clay pit or quarry

Refuse or slag heap

Sloping wall

☐ Water ☐ Mud

Sand; sand & shingle

National Park or Forest Park Boundary

NT National Trust open access

NT National Trust limited access

NTS NTS National Trust for Scotland

VEGETATION   Limits of vegetation are defined by positioning of the symbols but may be delineated also by pecks or dots

Coniferous trees

Non-coniferous trees

Coppice

Orchard

Scrub

Marsh, reeds, saltings

Bracken, rough grassland

In some areas bracken ( ) and rough grassland ( ) are shown separately

Heath

Shown collectively as rough grassland on some sheets

In some areas reeds ( ) and saltings ( ) are shown separately

HEIGHTS AND ROCK FEATURES

50 ⎫ Determined ⎧ ground survey
285 ⎭ by ⎩ air survey

Surface heights are to the nearest metre above
mean sea level. Heights shown close to a
triangulation pillar refer to the ground level
height at the pillar and not necessarily the summit.

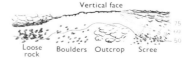

Vertical face

Loose rock Boulders Outcrop Scree

Contours are at
5 metres
vertical interval

TOURIST INFORMATION

✠ Abbey, Cathedral, Priory

🐟 Aquarium

⛺ Camp site

🚐 Caravan site

🏰 Castle

Cave

Country park

Craft centre

P Parking

PC Public Convenience (in rural areas)

ℳ Ancient Monuments and Historic Buildings in the care of the Secretary of State for the Environment which are open to the public.

◆━━◆ National trail or Recreational Path Long Distance Route (Scotland only)

Pennine Way   Named path

Garden

Golf course or links

Historic house

Information centre

Motor racing

Museum

Nature or forest trail

Nature reserve

Castle
SAILING   Selected places of interest

T Public telephone

⊕ Mountain rescue post

NATIONAL PARK Boundary of National Park access land
ACCESS LAND Private land for which the National Park Planning Board have negotiated public access

◄ Access Point

☆ Other tourist feature

✕ Picnic site

Preserved railway

Racecourse

Skiing

Viewpoint

Wildlife park

Zoo

WALKS

🔍**1** Start point of walk   Featured walk   ➡ Route of walk   ▪▪-)▪- Alternative route

---

ABBREVIATIONS   1:25 000 or 2½ INCHES to 1 MILE also 1:10 000/1:10 560 or 6 INCHES to 1 MILE

BP,BS	Boundary Post or Stone	P	Post Office	A,R	Telephone, AA or RAC
CH	Club House	Pol Sta	Police Station	TH	Town Hall
F V	Ferry Foot or Vehicle	PC	Public Convenience	Twr	Tower
FB	Foot Bridge	PH	Public House	W	Well
HO	House	Sch	School	Wd Pp	Wind Pump
MP,MS	Mile Post or Stone	Spr	Spring		
Mon	Monument	T	Telephone, public		

Abbreviations applicable only to 1:10 000/1:10 560 or 6 INCHES to 1 MILE

Ch	Church	GP	Guide Post	TCB	Telephone Call Box
F Sta	Fire Station	P	Pole or Post	TCP	Telephone Call Post
Fn	Fountain	S	Stone	Y	Youth Hostel

FOLLOW THE COUNTRY CODE
Enjoy the countryside and respect its life and work

Guard against all risk of fire

Fasten all gates

Keep your dogs under close control

Keep to public paths across farmland

Leave livestock, crops and machinery alone

Use gates and stiles to cross fences, hedges and walls

Take your litter home

Help to keep all water clean

Protect wildlife, plants and trees

Take special care on country roads

Make no unnecessary noise

Reproduced by permission of the Countryside Commission

1 Newland

Start:	Newland
Distance:	3½ miles (5·5 km)
Approximate time:	2 hours
Parking:	Near church at Newland
Refreshments:	Pub at Newland
Ordnance Survey maps:	Landranger 162 (Gloucester & Forest of Dean) and Outdoor Leisure 14 (Wye Valley & Forest of Dean)

General description This easy walk combines pleasant scenery – an appealing mixture of woodland and pasture – with a chance to visit one of the most attractive villages in the Forest of Dean. From Newland the walk descends through woods into a beautiful, quiet, remote valley, following it in an anti-clockwise direction as it curves round in a horseshoe shape, before climbing back to the village.

Most of the forest villages are predominantly nineteenth-century mining settlements with few architectural pretensions but Newland is a much older agricultural community with a superb thirteenth- to fourteenth-century church, aptly described as the 'Cathedral of the Forest'; the distinguished seventeenth- and eighteenth-century houses around it provide a setting reminiscent of a cathedral close. It is an unusually large, wide and handsome building for such a small village but the original parish included a number of smaller settlements, like Bream and Coleford, that later grew into larger industrial communities. The chief glory of the church is the ornate tower which dominates the village and much of the surrounding area.

Start by the pub and church by going through the lych-gate and walking across the churchyard to pass through another gate at the far end. At the T-junction turn left down a steep, narrow lane, turn right at another T-junction (**A**), and where the tarmac lane ends continue along a stony track, enclosed by trees and hedges, which gently ascends to reach a junction of tracks and paths (**B**).

Keep straight ahead to descend some

```
0    200   400   600   800 m   1        Kilometres
|----|----|----|----|----|----|              SCALE 1:25 000 or 2½ INCHES to 1 MILE
0    200   400   600   800   1000 yds   Miles   1
```

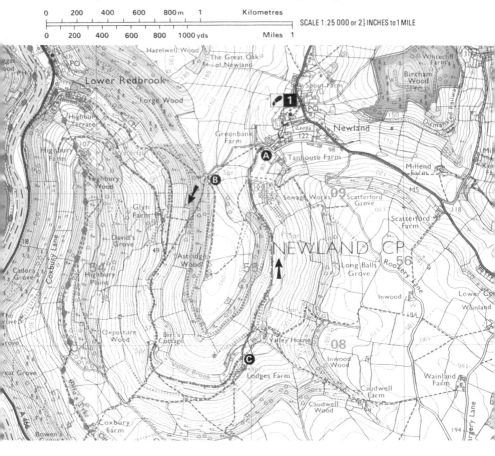

Newland church, the 'Cathedral of the Forest'

steps and follow a narrow downhill path through thick woodland to a track. Cross over and continue along the path, which bears left and drops down to a gate. Go through, keep ahead along a faint path that heads downhill across a field to join a broad track by a metal gate and turn left to pass through the gate. Now follow the track through the quiet, remote valley of Valley Brook below wooded slopes on both sides, at first with the brook on the right, passing through a series of metal gates, and later crossing the brook to continue with it on the left. Where the stony track bears right to a farmhouse keep ahead, go through a metal gate and continue along a grassy track which curves to the left around the head of the

valley — a most pleasant part of the walk — keeping above the brook on the left all the while.

Go through a metal gate and continue, still curving gradually to the left and climbing two fences in quick succession just below farm buildings on the right — there are no proper stiles but the fences are low and easy to get over. Keep ahead to climb another low fence and then bear left to join a track (**C**). Cross the brook, pass through a metal gate and continue along the track for 1 mile (1·5 km) — after a short while the prominent tower of Newland church comes into sight. The track later becomes a tarmac lane and continues to a T-junction where you turn right to retrace your steps uphill back into the village.

2 White Castle

Start:	White Castle
Distance:	3 miles (4·75 km)
Approximate time:	1½ hours
Parking:	Near entrance to White Castle
Refreshments:	Pub at Llanvetherine
Ordnance Survey maps:	Landranger 161 (Abergavenny & the Black Mountains) and Pathfinder 1086, SO 21/31 (Abergavenny)

General description From the ridge occupied by the White Castle the walk descends into the valley of the River Trothy to the small village of Llanvetherine, returning via a parallel route. The scenery in this part of the Welsh border country is superb − a lovely patchwork of rolling hills, fields and hedgerows, and small belts of woodland. The views are expansive and there are just two short, modest climbs.

White Castle is one of the 'Trilateral' castles of Gwent − the other two are Skenfrith and Grosmont − built to protect this area of the Welsh Marches, and it occupies a fine vantage point high above the valley of the little River Trothy looking towards the Black Mountains. The original twelfth-century fortress was considerably strengthened and enlarged in the thirteenth century when Welsh power was being consolidated by Llywelyn ap Gruffydd, but his defeat and the subsequent conquest of Wales by Edward I removed the threat and White Castle had a largely uneventful history. Its name comes from the coating of white plaster that originally covered the stonework. The castle covers a large area and its curtain walls, rounded towers and elaborate earthworks make an impressive and formidable sight.

From the parking area take the path signposted to Pont Gilbert, with an Offa's Dyke Path waymark, along the left-hand side of woodland, following the line of the castle walls. Climb a stile beside a metal

White Castle

16

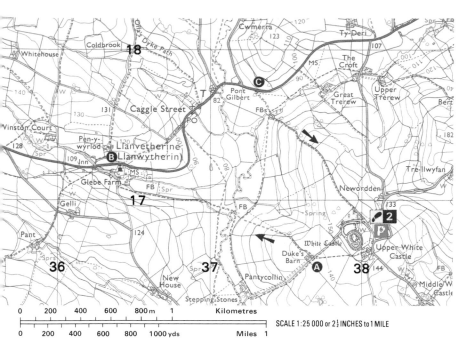

```
0    200   400   600   800 m   1        Kilometres
|--|--|--|--|--|--|--|--|--|
0    200   400   600   800   1000 yds            Miles  1
```
SCALE 1:25 000 or 2½ INCHES to 1 MILE

gate and bear right along the right-hand edge of a field, by a hedge on the right. Just before reaching the end of the field, turn right over a stile at an Offa's Dyke Path signpost (**A**). Keep ahead along the left-hand edge of a field, passing a barn on the left, soon bearing left over a stile and then bearing right to continue along the right-hand edge of a field, by a hedge on the right.

Follow the field edge as it curves left to a stile, climb over, bear half-left and head downhill across a large, sloping field — there are magnificent panoramic views from here dominated by the distinctive shape of Ysgyryd Fawr — making for a waymarked stile about halfway along the bottom end of the field. Climb over and keep ahead to cross a footbridge over the River Trothy. At this point you leave Offa's Dyke Path and continue across the field ahead — there is no obvious path — making for another footbridge on the left-hand side just before the end of the field.

Cross the footbridge, keep ahead a few yards and then turn right along the right-hand edge of a field, by a hedge on the right. Go through a metal gate, continue along the right-hand edge of the next field, which is likely to be overgrown, and soon the tower of Llanvetherine church comes into view. Continue, past a barn on the right, to a stile by a metal gate at the far end of the field, climb the stile and turn right along a broad, hedge-lined track. Cross a footbridge, climb a stone stile to enter the churchyard, and bear left across a corner of it, going through a gate

on the left. Continue along a grassy path by a house on the right, go through another gate, cross another footbridge and follow the track ahead to emerge onto a road beside the pub.

Turn right and opposite the church gates turn left over a stile at a footpath sign (**B**). The next part of the walk is likely to be overgrown. Turn half-right and head diagonally uphill across a field, making for the top corner and the end of a line of trees. Just beyond the trees go through a gate and continue straight across the next field. Climb a stile and keep ahead along the top left-hand edge of the next field, by a hedge and line of trees on the left, heading downhill to climb a stile beside a metal gate. Continue down the tarmac track, passing houses on the left, into the hamlet of Caggle Street. Bear left on rejoining the road and keep along it, passing a chapel on the left and curving right over a bridge, Pont Gilbert.

Just before the road turning to the left, turn right over a stile at a public footpath sign to White Castle (**C**) to follow a faint, narrow and rather overgrown path across a field towards the trees in front. Cross a footbridge over a brook, bear right and head up to climb a stile. Now turn left and continue uphill along the left-hand edge of several fields, keeping by a wire fence or hedge on the left all the while, passing over several stiles, through gates and enjoying more fine panoramic views. Finally follow a sunken, grassy track lined with oaks to a stile on the edge of woodland. Climb it and continue along the left-hand edge of the wood back to the starting point.

3 Newent and Acorn Wood

Start:	Newent
Distance:	5 miles (8 km)
Approximate time:	2½ hours
Parking:	Newent
Refreshments:	Pubs and cafés at Newent
Ordnance Survey maps:	Landranger 162 (Gloucester & Forest of Dean) and Pathfinder 1065, SO 62/72 (Ross-on-Wye (East))

General description *This is a gentle walk in the orchard and arable country that lies between the Severn and Wye valleys on the north-eastern fringes of the Forest of Dean. As much of it is across fairly flat and open terrain, there are wide and extensive views: southwards to the wooded slopes of the forest, and northwards, rather further away, to the distinctive outline of the Malvern Hills.*

Despite recent suburban development and its proximity to the M50, Newent retains the air of a traditional, sleepy old market town. A mixture of pleasant but unpretentious buildings of several ages, some timber-framed and others with dignified eighteenth-century brick frontages, line its streets, and in

the town centre stands the half-timbered, early seventeenth-century Market House. Nearby is the church, a slightly confusing building of medieval origin but with a nave that was rebuilt in the 1670s following a collapse. Its imposing tower and spire dominate both the town and much of the surrounding countryside.

The walk begins by the library, opposite the car park. Start by walking away from the town centre for a few yards and turn left along Watery Lane. On reaching a recreation ground turn right (**A**) along its right-hand edge, by a hedge and fence on the right, to the far end. Keep ahead along a short stretch of road between houses and then continue along a narrow path, between garden fencing on the left and a wire fence on the right, to a lane.

Turn left along this lane for ¼ mile (0·5 km) and where it bends to the left in front of a thatched cottage (**B**) keep ahead along a track and go through a metal gate. Continue, passing by a house and nurseries on the left, and the track becomes a narrow path which leads between a row of trees on the right and a wire fence on the left to a gate. Go through, continue along a tarmac drive and bear right to pass through a metal gate onto a lane. Turn left and take the first turning on the right (**C**), along the drive to Knappers Farm. There are splendid views ahead of the sylvan heights of Newent Woods, on the northern edge of the forest. Go through a metal gate, pass in front of the farmhouse on the right and continue through another metal gate, bearing slightly right to

The gentle countryside around Newent

go through a third one. Now turn right along the edge of a field and after about 50 yards (46 m) turn left along a track and follow it straight across a field. Continue along the left-hand edge of the next field, by a hedge on the left, and at the end of that field go through the left-hand one of two metal gates to enter Acorn Wood.

Continue through this pleasant woodland, taking the right-hand path at a fork after a few yards. The path climbs gently and later flattens out to reach a metal gate; go through the turn left (**D**) along a tarmac drive in front of a house. Where the drive curves to the left, keep ahead along a track which gently descends, first curving right and finally curving left in front of a cottage to reach a lane.

Turn left along the lane for ½ mile (0·75 km), passing the entrance to the National Birds of Prey Centre. The hills ahead are the Malverns. Just after passing Boulsdon Croft, a large, brick-built house on the right, turn right (**E**) and head downhill across a field, between crops and fruit trees, to reach the bottom end opposite a footbridge over a brook. Do not cross this bridge but turn left to walk along the bottom edge of several fields, climbing stiles, passing through gates and keeping close to the brook on the right all the time. After passing a pond on the left descend slightly into the next field and after a few yards turn right to climb a half-hidden stile. Continue along the right-hand edge of a field, climb a stile, and carry on along the edge of the next field, bearing slightly left to a metal gate. Go through, keep ahead towards Brook Farm, go through another metal gate and then on through a wooden gate, passing in front of the farmhouse on the left.

Cross a lane and climb a stile into a field of rough grassland. Follow the brook on the right and pass through a metal gate. Continue across another area of rough grassland, bearing slightly left along the top edge of it, by a hedge on the left, to climb a stile. Keep by a wire fence that borders a playing field on the left, following the edge of the playing field around to the left and then turning right through a gate. Continue along a tarmac path, cross a road, and keep ahead along another tarmac path between gardens, following it to the right and up to a road. Turn left into Newent town centre, bearing left at a junction to return to the starting point.

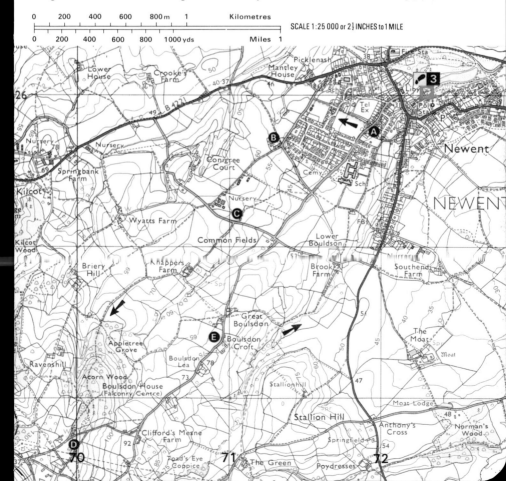

SCALE 1:25 000 or 2½ INCHES to 1 MILE

4 King's Caple, Sellack and Hoarwithy

Start: King's Caple church

Distance: 5 miles (8 km)

Approximate time: 2½ hours

Parking: Plenty of wide verges near King's Caple church

Refreshments: Pub at Hoarwithy

Ordnance Survey maps: Landrangers 149 (Hereford & Leominster) and 162 (Gloucester & Forest of Dean), Pathfinder 1064, SO 42/52 (Ross-on-Wye (West))

General description There can be few short walks more pleasant than this gentle stroll through one of the loveliest stretches of the Wye Valley that reveals English riverside scenery at its finest: an intimate patchwork of fields and orchards, rolling hills and woodland, delightful riverside meadows and quiet old villages. The route passes through three of the latter, each with highly distinctive churches, and for most of the way the spire of King's Caple church, the starting point, is in sight.

Start by King's Caple church, the first of three interesting and varied village churches that can be visited on this walk. A handsome building occupying a fine, elevated position above the valley, it is built of the local rich red sandstone. It is a harmonious mixture of styles, ranging mainly from the twelfth to the fifteenth centuries, and is dominated by the fourteenth-century tower and spire, a landmark for miles around. The mound on the opposite side of the road is 'Caple Tump', site of an early motte and bailey castle.

With your back to the church, turn left along the lane through the small village, passing an orchard on the right. Keep ahead at a crossroads and about 50 yards (46 km) after passing a school on the left, and a few yards after passing a public footpath sign on the left, turn right along a tarmac drive (**A**). Where that drive bears left up to a house continue along a hedge-lined track to go through a metal gate and climb a stile beside another metal gate a few yards ahead.

Bear slightly right and head across the field to a fence corner, here veering left to walk along the field edge, by a wire fence on the left, down to a stile. From here there are

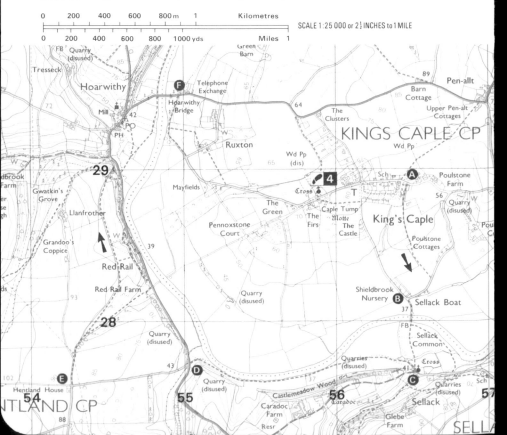

The Wye Valley near King's Caple

expansive views ahead over the Wye Valley with the spire of Sellack church prominent. Climb the stile, continue in the same direction along a narrow path, now by the right-hand edge of a field and with a wire fence and hedge on the right. Where the hedge and fence turn to the right, keep straight ahead across a cultivated field, turning left at the bottom end for a few yards to a metal gate and footpath sign. Go through the gate and turn right along a lane to where it bends to the right, here turning left (**B**) through a metal gate and on along a hedge-lined path to cross a rather shaky suspension bridge over the River Wye, built in 1895 to replace an earlier ford and ferry — hence the name Sellack Boat on the map.

Walk across the meadow ahead in the direction of Sellack church, crossing a footbridge over a ditch and continuing across this broad expanse of meadowland to go through a metal gate beside the church (**C**). This is another attractive old sandstone building with a fine fourteenth-century spire. The village is tiny and secluded, no more than a few houses and farms.

Immediately turn right through another metal gate and head across meadows, keeping more or less in a straight line and roughly parallel with the wooded cliff of Castlemeadow Wood on the left, to reach the riverbank a short distance before a stile. Climb the stile and keep along the riverbank; this is an idyllic part of the walk as the Wye flows serenely through a lush landscape of meadows, fields of green and gold, orchards, farms and villages, with rolling wooded hills beyond and church spires punctuating the skyline. Eventually you follow a path to the left by some cottages; look out for a stile on the right and climb it onto a road.

Turn left for a few yards and take the first turning on the right (**D**), signposted Kynaston and Hentland, following a road gently uphill for ½ mile (0·75 km) to where it bends sharply to the left. Here turn right (**E**), at a public footpath sign, along a hedge-lined track, and where the track bends left in front of a pylon keep ahead along a grassy

enclosed path, which may be overgrown, to a stile. Climb it and continue along the left-hand edge of a field, by a hedge and wire fence on the left. There are more superb views over the valley, with the spire of King's Caple church the dominant feature. Go through a metal gate and keep ahead, turning left over a stile about halfway along the edge of the next field.

Continue along the left-hand edge of a field, by a hedge and wire fence on the left — there is a grand view of the River Wye and the houses of Hoarwithy ahead. Follow the field edge as it curves gradually to the right to reach a rather broken-down gate, half hidden by trees and bushes. Go through it to a junction of tracks, keep straight ahead along a grassy track, passing to the left of a house called Quarry Bank, and continue downhill along a delightful, if in places overgrown, tree-enclosed path to a road. Follow the road through the village of Hoarwithy, bearing right at a junction in the direction of King's Caple.

To the left is Hoarwithy church, which you reach by climbing some steps. Its Italian design could hardly look more incongruous in this quintessentially English setting. The reason why such an unusual, highly ornate and richly decorated church came to be built here is that the local vicar, William Poole, felt that its predecessor was too plain and therefore used some of his great personal fortune to finance the construction of this lavish replacement in 1885. It took over twenty years to finish and Poole even employed Italian craftsmen to achieve the desired effect. One feature that it has in common with the churches at King's Caple and Sellack, however, is that it is built of the local sandstone.

Continue across the bridge over the Wye and on the other side turn right (**F**) along a grassy, hedge- and tree-lined track, which shortly meets and keeps by the river for a while, before curving left away from it to reach a lane. Follow the lane for nearly ¾ mile (1·25 km) back to King's Caple church.

5 Abbey Dore and Ewyas Harold

Start: Abbey Dore

Distance: 4½ miles (7·25 km)

Approximate time: 2½ hours

Parking: Roadside parking area by Dore Abbey

Refreshments: Pub at Abbey Dore, pubs at Ewyas Harold

Ordnance Survey maps: Landrangers 149 (Hereford & Leominster) and 161 (Abergavenny & the Black Mountains), Pathfinders 1063, SO 22/32, (Longtown & Pandy) and 1039, SO 23/33 (Golden Valley)

General description The name Golden Valley is really a misnomer; the little river that waters it is called the River Dore, and this name was thought by the Normans to be the same as the French d'or (golden) when in fact it is derived from the Welsh dwr meaning water. Misnomer or not, it is an apt name for this lovely, remote, fertile and peaceful valley, situated between the Wye Valley and Black Mountains, that really does look golden on a fine summer day. Starting from the remains of a historic abbey near the southern end of the valley, the route climbs over the open gorse and bracken expanses of Ewyas Harold Common to drop into the adjoining Dulas valley, and continues beside Dulas Brook before heading over the common again to descend back into the Golden Valley. From the breezy heights of the common there are glorious views over the Welsh border country.

The small, secluded village of Abbey Dore is grouped around the splendid remains of its once great Cistercian abbey, founded in 1120 and dissolved in 1535. After the dissolution it fell into ruin and the huge nave, 250 feet (76·2 m) long, entirely disappeared but the rest of the church was rescued and restored by its owner, Lord Scudamore, in the seventeenth century. Externally the result is an unusual but pleasing combination of the thirteenth-century east end and transepts and a seventeenth-century tower placed between the choir and south transept. Inside there is a fine contrast between the impressive and dignified simplicity of the original Early English architecture and the superb oak roof and carved screen from the seventeenth-century restoration.

The walk starts at the lych-gate of the abbey. Climb a half-hidden stile on the other side of the road and head uphill across a field in a straight line — there is no visible path — looking for a gap in the hedge in front. Here climb a fence (in the absence of a stile) and, bearing slightly left, continue uphill across the next field — again there is no path. On meeting a hedge turn left and keep beside it to go through a metal gate. Bear left in front of a house and then bear right (**A**) to follow a broad, grassy path across the open, breezy, bracken- and gorse-covered Ewyas Harold Common. As the common occupies a plateau, over 500 feet (152 m) high above the Golden and Dulas valleys, there are superb views all around, especially westwards looking to the line of the Black Mountains. Many paths criss-cross the common, which can be confusing, but head southwards, keeping roughly in a straight line and parallel to the trees bordering its left-hand edge.

On reaching a stony track in front of buildings, turn sharp right (**B**) along it and to the left you can see the village of Ewyas Harold nestling in the valley. After a short while turn sharply to the left off the stony track, almost doubling back, to continue downhill along a sandy track towards the

Abbey Dore nestling in the Golden Valley

village. The track bears right over a cattle grid, after which it becomes a tarmac lane, and continues down past modern houses. Do not turn right along Priors Field but take the next road on the right, passing a primary school on the left, and continue to a T-junction in the village centre, with pubs to both the left and right (**C**).

Turn right for a few yards and then right again, by Dulas Brook, up to the sturdy-looking thirteenth-century church. Pass through the churchyard — from here there is a view of the castle mound, all that remains of one of the earliest of Norman border fortresses — and go through a kissing-gate at the far end. Keep ahead through a metal gate to walk along the right-hand edge of a sports field, turn right over a stile and then turn left along the edge of a field, by a hedge and wire fence on the left. Pass through a gate and continue along a narrow, possibly overgrown, path that keeps along the right-hand edge of a field, by a hedge on the right. At the end of the field go through a metal gate and continue along an attractive broad track, by a hedge on the right and the tree-lined Dulas Brook to the left, towards another metal gate, but about 50 yards (46 m) before it turn right over a rather broken-down stile (**D**). Walk along the right-hand edge of a field, by a hedge on the right, climb another broken-down stile at the end and turn left to continue along a very pleasant enclosed track. Head uphill to a house, take the track that passes to the right of it, go through a metal gate and continue along a grassy track that curves to the left, keeping by a wire fence on the right, to a stile.

Climb it and turn right along a broad stony track a few yards ahead (**E**), turning right again at a T-junction to head once more across Ewyas Harold Common. Where the stony track bears left, keep ahead along a grassy track in an easterly direction. On seeing the chimneys of a house on the left, bear left towards the house, which lies on the edge of the common, here temporarily rejoining the outward route (**A**).

Bear left by the side of the house, go through the right-hand one of two metal gates and continue in a straight line, beside a hedge on the left. To the right is a magnificent view across the Golden Valley — a mixture of greens and golds, woodlands and fields, with Dore Abbey below forming the focal point of this glorious scene. Here leave the outward route by continuing straight ahead, the hedge on the left turning to the left after a while, making for and then keeping by the left-hand side of another hedge. Here pick up a discernible path again and after this hedge turns to the right keep ahead to pass through a metal gate. Continue between farm buildings, following a track

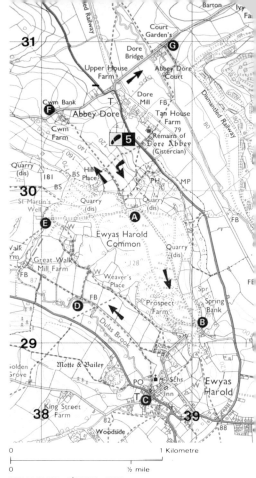

SCALE 1:25 000 or 2½ INCHES to 1 MILE

which bears right, passing a duck pond, to reach a lane (**F**).

Turn right along the lane, heading gently downhill into Abbey Dore, keep ahead at the first junction and continue to a second junction. Here you can turn right for a quick return to the start, but for a much pleasanter finale bear left along the lane signposted to Wormbridge and Kingstone, cross the placid River Dore and continue past Abbey Dore Court on the right. Just in front of a house on the left turn right (**G**) along a hedge-lined track and after about 100 yards (91 m), where the track bears left to a gate in a high wire fence, keep ahead to climb a stile.

Continue along a broad, grassy track which soon turns right, by a hedge on the right and the high wire fence on the left, shortly turning left to keep beside the river. Turn right over a footbridge to cross the river and bear left across a field, making towards the left-hand side of the abbey church in front. Go through a gate, keep ahead to pass through a metal kissing-gate and continue along a tarmac path through the churchyard to return to the starting point.

23

6 New Fancy and Mallards Pike Lake

Start:	Forestry Commission car park at New Fancy
Distance:	4 ½ miles (7·25 km)
Approximate time:	2 ½ hours
Parking:	New Fancy car park
Refreshments:	Pub at Moseley Green
Ordnance Survey maps:	Landranger 162 (Gloucester & Forest of Dean) and Outdoor Leisure 14 (Wye Valley & Forest of Dean)

General description *Quiet forest tracks and pleasant glades make it difficult to believe that most of this walk is in the vicinity of what was once a busy coal-mining area; it crosses several of the disused railway lines that served the nearby collieries. The route passes through mixed woodland, Mallards Pike Lake adds variety, and either at the beginning or the end you can enjoy an extensive panoramic view over the Forest of Dean from the top of the landscaped tip of the former New Fancy Colliery.*

The walk begins on the site of the New Fancy Colliery which opened in 1832 and closed in 1944. Between those years it produced around 3 ½ million tons of coal. The vast spoil heap was partially removed in 1961 and the rest was grassed over and landscaped in 1975 to form a car park, picnic site and viewpoint.

From the car park follow red-waymarked 'Forest Trail' signs, turning right along a track that was originally a colliery tramway. Climb a stile beside a gate, and at a T-junction turn left (**A**) along a track bordered by a now incomplete avenue of lime trees that were planted in the early nineteenth century. Keep ahead at a junction to cross the former 'Mineral Loop' line of the Severn & Wye Valley Railway Company, opened in 1872 to serve the local collieries. The line was at its peak just before the First World War, declined in the 1920s and '30s and finally closed in 1953.

Continue along the pleasant straight track to the next crossroads and here cross the track of a railway line that was abandoned before even being completed. This was the Forest of Dean Central Railway, a competitor of the Severn & Wye company, and it was because the latter's 'Mineral Loop' line won the lucrative trade of the New Fancy Colliery that the Central railway stopped laying its track.

Keep straight ahead along a narrow path that heads uphill to a crossroads of paths (**B**). Turn right, head down to another crossroads, continue along a path – following yellow waymarks – that winds downhill and just after it starts to ascend bear left at a yellow waymark. Head gently uphill again, cross a track and continue through the conifers, crossing over another track and now climbing more steeply to reach a track at the top of the hill in front of Staple-edge Bungalows (**C**).

Turn right along the broad main track – there are several routes here which can be slightly confusing – and on reaching the corner of the wire fence bordering the bungalow garden on the left, bear right off this main track along a pleasant grassy path.

The splendid view over the Forest of Dean from the landscaped tip of the former New Fancy Colliery

The path continues gently downhill, keeping more or less in a straight line, through a conifer plantation and over several cross-roads of paths to reach a broad track (**D**). Turn right along it and at a T-junction of tracks turn sharp left (**E**), almost doubling back and heading downhill. The track passes the attractive, tree-fringed Mallards Pike Lake below on the right, created by the Forestry Commission in 1982 as a recreational amenity. Continue over a disused railway line in a cutting below, pass by a forestry barrier and keep ahead to a road.

Cross over and take the track straight ahead, passing by another forestry barrier, and follow it as far as a junction of tracks just in front of a telegraph pole (**F**). Here turn sharp right along a grassy track which continues to the road at Moseley Green almost opposite the Rising Sun Inn. Turn right for a few yards and then turn left along another broad, grassy track, passing a forestry barrier and heading uphill. Keep in a straight line all the while — at first through conifers and later through a delightful and extensive area of broad-leaved woodland — to reach a road junction (**G**).

Take the road ahead, signposted to Speech House and Cinderford, turning along the first track on the right. Climb a stile beside a gate and continue along the track as far as a red-waymarked post where you turn left (**A**) to retrace your steps to New Fancy car park. If you did not do so at the start, climb up to the viewpoint on top of the former colliery spoil heap to take in the magnificent all-round panorama over the densely wooded forest.

SCALE 1:25 000 or 2½ INCHES to 1 MILE

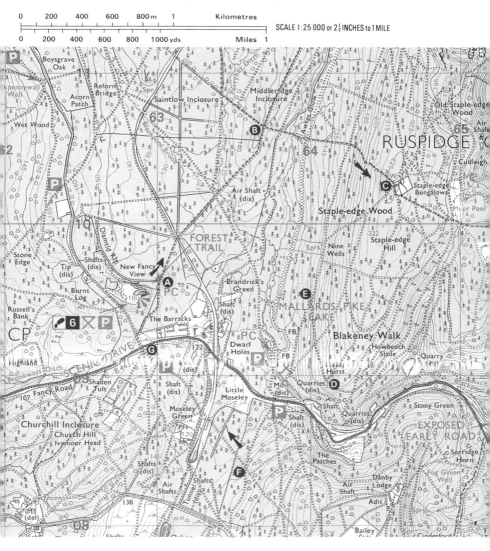

7 Wynd Cliff

Start:	Forestry Commission car park at Upper Wyndcliff
Distance:	4 miles (6·5 km)
Approximate time:	2 hours
Parking:	Upper Wyndcliff car park
Refreshments:	None
Ordnance Survey maps:	Landranger 162 (Gloucester & Forest of Dean) and Outdoor Leisure 14 (Wye Valley & Forest of Dean)

General description *This walk has two contrasting halves. The first half formed part of the 'Grand Tour' of the Wye Valley area during the Romantic period; it heads steeply down and then up the thickly wooded Wynd Cliff on the west bank of the river, follows the most delightful paths that wind between rocks and trees, and passes some superlative viewpoints. After a section along a rocky and* rather overgrown track, the second half of the walk is a pleasant stroll along quiet lanes that give more open, if less dramatic, views.

The first part of the route is the 'Wyndcliff Walk' — a popular excursion for the Romantics, the collective name for the poets, writers, artists and gentlemen of leisure who liked to come here during the Romantic period in the eighteenth and nineteenth centuries when it became fashionable to explore what were considered wild and untamed places, such as this part of the Wye Valley. Noticeboards provide details of the history, geology and flora of the locality.

From the car park do not take the main path, which is signposted 'Eagles Nest, Wye Valley Walk and 365 Steps', unless you wish to avoid the descent and ascent of the Wynd Cliff — you rejoin this path later just before it reaches the Eagles Nest viewpoint. Instead take the pleasant, broad, well-constructed path waymarked with yellow arrows and red dots that heads immediately into the woods and winds downhill, over a stile and into Wyndcliff Quarry car park, an open area below the cliffs. Here turn right down to the main Chepstow – Monmouth road (**A**), cross

The Wye gorge and the Severn estuary and bridge from the Wynd Cliff

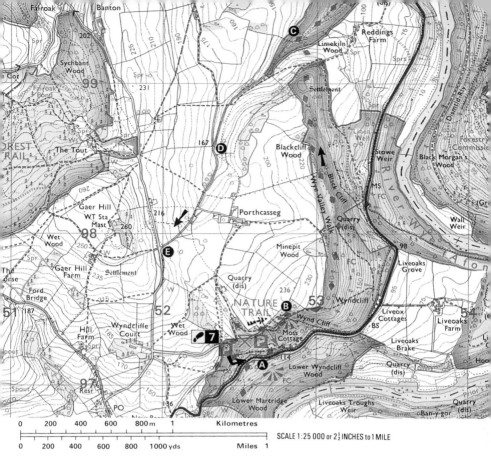

```
0    200   400   600   800m    1
|--|--|--|--|--|--|--|--|--|--------|
0    200   400   600   800  1000 yds
```
Kilometres

SCALE 1:25 000 or 2½ INCHES to 1 MILE

```
|--|--|--|--|--|--|--|--|--|--------|
Miles 1
```

it − take care as it is a busy road and visibility is not good at this point − and continue through the Lower Wyndcliff car park to the trees, from where there is a lovely viewpoint over the winding river.

Return to the quarry and turn right for the most spectacular, although only moderately strenuous, section of the walk. Follow a winding, rocky path through outstandingly attractive woodland to the base of the '365 Steps' and then ascend them. As you proceed upwards it is easy to appreciate why the Romantics would have loved this wonderfully picturesque combination of rocks, gnarled and twisted trees and the perpendicular towering limestone cliff. Take care, for although there is a handrail, in places the rocky steps can be slippery. At one stage you ascend a wooden staircase before reaching the top where you turn right, at an 'Eagles Nest Viewpoint' signpost, to join the Wye Valley Walk (**B**). Keep ahead along the top edge of the woods, turning right and heading down some steps to reach the viewpoint. The Eagles Nest viewing platform is a few yards to the right and from it a magnificent vista unfolds over the great meanders in the Wye around Lancaut, the almost perpendicular wooded cliffs near

Wintour's Leap, Chepstow, the Severn Bridge and estuary and the Cotswolds on the horizon.

Continue through the woods following the Wye Valley Walk − the path later turns sharply right, drops steeply downhill, soon curves left and continues downhill, curving to the right and left again and descending to a stile on the edge of the woods. Climb over, turn left along the left-hand edge of the woods, soon turning right, at a Wye Valley Walk waymark, across a field and heading down to climb a stile on the edge of more woodland. Turn left along a path that continues downhill through the trees, bearing right to meet a track. Here leave the Wye Valley Walk by turning left (**C**) along this enclosed track, which is narrow, rough, rocky and overgrown in places, heading gently uphill to emerge onto a narrow lane (**D**).

Bear left along the lane for ½ mile (0·75 km), climbing steadily to a T-junction (**E**). Turn left along another lane for ½ mile (0·75 km), with fine views across to Chepstow and the Severn estuary, and descend to a crossroads. Here turn left back to the Forestry Commission car park at Upper Wyndcliff.

8 Chepstow and Lancaut

Start:	Chepstow
Distance:	4 ½ miles (7·25 km)
Approximate time:	2 hours
Parking:	Chepstow
Refreshments:	Pubs and cafés at Chepstow
Ordnance Survey maps:	Landranger 162 (Gloucester & Forest of Dean) and Outdoor Leisure 14 (Wye Valley & Forest of Dean)

General description *From the gatehouse of Chepstow Castle the walk follows a*

dramatic stretch of the Wye upstream to where the river makes a great curve around the Lancaut peninsula; it returns via a high-level route which passes the spectacular viewpoint of Wintour's Leap. The walk is short enough to allow plenty of time to explore the medieval castle and walls of Chepstow, one of the finest border strongholds. There is one difficult section below Wintour's Leap where the path is narrow and rocky as it heads down to the riverbank.

Chepstow stands at the first bridging point over the Wye not far from where it disgorges into the Severn estuary. The town is dominated by the ruins of its mighty castle which occupy a fine strategic site on a sloping cliff above the river. Chepstow Castle was both one of the earliest stone castles and the first Norman castle in Wales. Begun in

Chepstow Castle — formidable border stronghold

1067 by William Fitz Osbern, Earl of Hereford, it was rebuilt and enlarged over the following centuries to create the present imposing structure. Particularly impressive are the Great Tower (the original enormous eleventh-century Norman keep, later reconstructed), the thirteenth-century Great Gatehouse and the powerful, rounded thirteenth-century Marten's Tower guarding the most vulnerable side of the castle. Additional attractions in the town are the medieval walls, much of which survive, and the church, which was once part of a Benedictine priory and although heavily restored retains a fine Norman doorway.

From the car park by the castle entrance turn left along the road, cross the bridge over the Wye, and where the road bends to the left keep ahead through a metal barrier and along an uphill tarmac track enclosed by walls. Halfway up you join Offa's Dyke Path. Climb some steps to reach a road, cross it, continue along the lane ahead and where it bends slightly to the right turn left over a stile into a field (**A**), at an Offa's Dyke Path acorn waymark. Walk gently uphill, passing the remains of a lookout tower, an outlying part of Chepstow's defences, on the right, making for a stile at the far end of this long, narrow, tapering field.

Turn right over the stile to continue along the left-hand edge of a field, by a wall on the left, turning left over a stile in the wall and continuing along an enclosed path. Turn right along a tarmac drive and after a few yards turn left over a stile and head across the middle of a field to climb another stile (**B**).

Here Offa's Dyke Path continues to the right but you keep ahead, passing under a footbridge to enter Lancaut Nature Reserve, and follow a path that heads downhill through thick woodland, below sheer cliffs on the right and above the broad river on the left. At this point both banks of the river are steep-sided and thickly wooded and there are grand views ahead approaching a great left-hand bend in the Wye. The next part of the walk is the awkward section: the path continues below a disused quarry and is overgrown and narrow in places. At one stage you have to clamber across fallen boulders — the route over these is indicated by yellow arrows painted on them — before continuing through trees and eventually descending to the riverbank.

Follow the river around the left-hand bend below the well-known viewpoint of Wintour's Leap — this is passed later — along an undulating and still wooded path, which is waymarked in places, keeping by the river until the path curves right to a metal stile. Climb it and take the path ahead which turns right at a yellow-waymarked post and continues uphill along the right-hand edge of

rough meadowland, by a wire fence on the right, passing the rather forlorn and neglected ruins of the abandoned Norman church at Lancaut, standing amidst its overgrown churchyard in which a few gravestones can still be seen. Go through a gap in the trees ahead and continue uphill across another rough field, keeping to the right of the farm buildings of Lancaut, and at the top of the field go through a metal gate and turn right along a lane (**C**). Follow this lane for nearly ¾ mile (1·25 km) through more attractive woodland — there are fine views later over both the Severn and the Wye — to join the Coleford-Chepstow road (**D**).

Turn sharp right, rejoining the route of Offa's Dyke Path, and at a left-hand bend there is a magnificent view over the Wye from Wintour's Leap looking across to the Wynd Cliff. The name comes from Sir John Wintour who is alleged to have jumped from here to escape from Parliamentary forces in 1642. Continue along the road, looking out for a waymark and finger-post for Sedbury Cliff where you bear right along a narrow path that passes the backs of houses and continues along a virtual clifftop above the Wye, giving more glorious views over the river far below. Go through a metal kissing-gate and keep above a huge disused quarry, later passing in front of a bungalow and continuing along a pleasant enclosed path. Go through two metal kissing-gates in quick succession and head downhill, curving left to pass through another metal kissing-gate and under an arch — the lintel of which says 'Medieval Times, Donkey Lane' — onto a road (**E**).

Turn sharp right — there is a good view of the Severn Bridge from here — and shortly turn right again through a metal kissing-gate and under another arch to continue along a narrow path, between a wall on the right and a metal fence and beyond that a field on the left. Turn left over a stile to rejoin the outward route (**B**) and retrace your steps to Chepstow, enjoying some fine views over the castle and town towards the end.

9 Mordiford and Haugh Wood

Start:	The bridge at Mordiford
Distance:	6 miles (9·5 km)
Approximate time:	3 hours
Parking:	Parking area on west side of Mordiford Bridge
Refreshments:	Pub at Mordiford
Ordnance Survey maps:	Landranger 149 (Hereford & Leominster) and Pathfinder 1040, SO 43/53 (Hereford (South) & area)

General description From the small riverside village of Mordiford the walk follows a gentle and easy route across fields, by orchards and along quiet lanes before climbing through the mixed woodlands of Haugh Wood. The wood, now owned and managed by the Forestry Commission but once belonging to Hereford Cathedral, makes pleasant walking, although there are a few short stretches of narrow and overgrown paths to negotiate before descending along a lane back into Mordiford. From the higher points on the walk there are fine views over the Wye Valley.

The village of Mordiford forms a most attractive composition when viewed from the old bridge over the River Lugg. Its half-timbered buildings rise serenely above the water-meadows, presided over by the tower of the medieval church and backed by the dark green slopes of Haugh Wood. Start by crossing the bridge, pass by the church on the left and turn right by the side of the post office (**A**). The first part of the walk is along a section of the Wye Valley Walk and is clearly waymarked. Cross a brook, turn left to follow a track up to a road, cross over and keep ahead through the yard of a former mill. Go through a metal gate, continue along the right-hand edge of a field, by a hedge on the right, and at the end of the field climb a stile and bear right through an orchard, still with the hedge on the right. Climb another stile and continue along a hedge-enclosed path, bearing left in front of houses to join a track.

Turn right at a crossroads of tracks, walk through a farmyard and keep ahead along a clear and broad track, from which there are pleasant views to the right across fields to low wooded hills. After passing through a metal gate, continue along a grassy path, more or less in a straight line, to a stile. Climb it and follow a rather indistinct path straight across the middle of a field, later joining a hedge and wire fence on the left and keeping by them to head gently downhill, eventually curving left to a lane (**B**).

Turn left along the lane, at this point leaving the Wye Valley Walk, and make a brief detour to the right through a metal gate where you see a sign 'Tom Spring Memorial'. The memorial lies just across the field and was erected in 1954 to commemorate the exploits of Thomas Winter, alias Tom Spring. Born nearby in 1795, he was the landlord of the Green Man at Fownhope and a renowned boxer, becoming champion of England. Return to the lane and shortly afterwards turn left (**C**) at a footpath sign beside a cottage, along a track into Haugh Wood. At a forestry barrier turn right along a broad uphill track and just after passing a track on the right turn left along another broad track. Almost immediately turn half-right onto an uphill path, keep to the right at a fork and continue along a very pleasant grassy path through lovely woodland, curving steadily to the right all the while and eventually bearing right to reach a T-junction of tracks.

Turn left here, at the next fork keep to the left along the main track, and at a T-junction a few yards ahead bear right along a grassy track. The track bears right, later narrows to a path and continues through conifers. On joining another path bear right and follow it as far as a crossroads; here turn left along a broad, sandy track and pass through a gap to the side of a forestry gate to come out onto the road opposite Haugh Wood car park (**D**).

Cross over, keep to the left of the car park and go through a forestry barrier to continue straight ahead along another broad, sandy track. At the first junction of tracks turn left and head gently downhill, keeping ahead at a crossroads. At this point there are lovely views ahead across the Wye Valley to the Black Mountains on the horizon. The track curves to the right and shortly afterwards you turn sharp left along a narrow path (**E**) — look out for it carefully as it is difficult to spot. It could also be difficult to negotiate as it is likely to be muddy and overgrown. Follow the path as it bears right and later, at a fork, bears left, to reach a gate in front of a house. Go through the gate, pass to the left of the house and bear right along a track which leads down to a lane. Turn right to follow the lane downhill into Mordiford, enjoying grand views all the way across the valley with the tower of Hereford Cathedral visible. At a T-junction bear right to walk through the village, passing the pub and church on the right, and recross the bridge to return to the starting point.

Mordiford church and bridge below the wooded slopes of Haugh Wood

SCALE 1:25 000 or 2½ INCHES to 1 MILE

10 Hay-on-Wye, Mouse Castle Wood and Cusop

Start:	Hay-on-Wye
Distance:	6 miles (9·5 km). Shorter version 4 miles (6·5 km)
Approximate time:	3 hours (2 hours for shorter version)
Parking:	Hay-on-Wye
Refreshments:	Pubs and cafés at Hay-on-Wye
Ordnance Survey maps:	Landrangers 148 (Presteigne & Hay-on-Wye) and 161 (Abergavenny & the Black Mountains), Pathfinder 1016, SO 24/34 (Hay-on-Wye)

General description *Starting from Hay-on-Wye, this pleasant and easy-paced walk goes across fields, through woods and by riverside meadows in the gentle rolling countryside of the Wye Valley immediately below the northern slopes of the Black Mountains. This is very much 'Kilvert Country': the village of Clyro, where he was curate for seven years, is only 1 mile (1·5 km) away and much of the route would have been familiar to him. The shorter version returns directly to Hay; the full walk includes an attractive open area called the Warren and a lovely final stretch by the placid Wye along the Bailey Walk, a popular local footpath.*

In many ways Hay-on-Wye looks a typical border town, with its narrow, winding streets rising from the river and its buildings huddled around the ruins of the castle. Closer acquaintance reveals that in at least two ways it is anything but typical. For a start the castle ruins are mostly those of a large seventeenth-century house built on the site of a medieval fortress, of which only fragments remain. Secondly, and more obviously, the town nowadays seems to be almost one gigantic second-hand bookshop, the result of the activities of Richard Booth, self styled 'King of Hay', who established his first bookshop in the castle and has subsequently expanded to take over many other properties for the same purpose.

Begin by turning right out of the car park along the road and after 100 yards (91 m) turn right again, at an Offa's Dyke Path sign, through a gate and along a track. Go through a metal kissing-gate into a field and continue along its left-hand edge, by a hedge and wire

fence on the left. Just before reaching the end of the field turn left over a stile and walk along the left-hand edge of the next field, climbing another stile to the left of a bungalow. Keep ahead for a few yards, turn left in front of a row of cottages to join a road, turn sharp right along it (**A**) and follow it for just over ¾ mile (1·25 km). Ahead are the thickly wooded slopes of Mouse Castle Wood.

Just beyond the drive of Hillswood Cottage on the right, turn right (**B**) over a stile (to the right of a gate) and head uphill along the right-hand edge of a field, by a ditch and line of trees on the right, towards the wood. Bear slightly left at the top end of the field to climb a stile into the wood and follow a steep, narrow, uphill path through it, keeping to the right at a fork and continuing uphill through dense woodland to reach a metal gate on the left. From the gate there is a lovely view across the Wye Valley. Do not go through it but keep ahead for about 100 yards (91 m), looking out carefully for a fork, which is not very clear and could easily be missed. Here turn right uphill, soon bearing left to continue along the top right-hand edge of Hawks Wood, by a wire fence to the right and beyond that an open field, to a gate.

Go through it, and through a metal gate a few yards ahead, and turn right (**C**) to keep along the right-hand edge of a field, by a wire fence and hedge on the right. To the left are glorious views looking towards the northern foothills of the Black Mountains. At the end of the field climb a stile onto a narrow lane and turn left. To the right can be seen the tree-covered motte of Mouse Castle, which features in Kilvert's diaries. Follow the twisting lane downhill and after a particularly sharp bend to the right you reach a footpath sign. Turn very sharply to the right onto a narrow path which bears left to a gate, go through and bear left again along a narrow and possibly overgrown path, by a wire fence on the left, initially through woodland. Turn left through another gate to continue along the edge of the woodland on the right, and ahead is a superb view of Hay backed by the hills of mid-Wales.

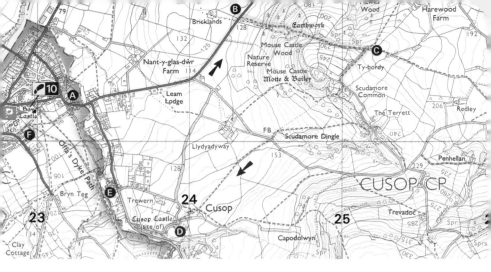

After a few yards bear left across a field – there is no visible path – and pass through a gap in the hedge in front. Continue in the same direction across the next field – Mouse Castle Wood is now over to the right – making for the corner of a fence. Here go through a metal gate and continue in a straight line along the left-hand edge of a field – the fence on the left tends to be irregular but head gently downhill to rejoin it and then continue by it downhill and to the left, crossing a brook and heading up to a stile. Climb the stile, cross a lane, climb another stile opposite and continue straight across the field ahead, later keeping by a hedge and wire fence on the left, to go through a metal gate.

Continue in the same direction across the next field, bearing away from the hedge on the right and making towards the house seen ahead. Go through a kissing-gate by a finger-post to enter Cusop churchyard, dominated by the huge, ancient yew tree near the south porch of the church and with a pleasantly remote and peaceful atmosphere. The church blends in with its surroundings perfectly; it is a small, simple building dating from the twelfth century and retains a fine Norman chancel arch.

Walk past the church to go through the lych-gate and keep straight ahead (D) along a narrow lane – the mound in the field on the left is all that remains of Cusop Castle. Follow the lane, which bears right and heads downhill through trees to join another lane. Bear right along this through Cusop village and just after passing a road junction on the right turn left (E) by the side of a house called Rose Dale. Soon bear right, at a 'Footbridge' sign, along a tarmac track and head downhill. Cross a footbridge, continue between cottages and climb some steps to go through a metal kissing-gate. Head across a field to another kissing-gate in a wall on the right, go through it (to briefly join Offa's Dyke Path)

and keep along the left-hand edge of a field, by a wire fence on the left. Hay-on-Wye is directly in front. Go through a metal kissing-gate, turn half-left and head diagonally across a field, passing through another metal kissing-gate and on across the next field in the corner of which are two more kissing-gates (F).

At this point, those wishing to do only the shorter version of the walk can go through the right-hand kissing-gate, which leads directly into the car park.

Go through the left-hand one and along a narrow, tarmac, hedge-lined path, passing through a metal kissing-gate and down steps onto a road. Turn right to a T-junction, turn right again for a few yards, and just before a row of almshouses turn left along a narrow path. Cross a brook, turn right to recross it and walk beside it to go through a metal kissing-gate onto a road. To the right is a motte, the site of Hay's original castle. Turn left along the road for just over ¼ mile (0·5 km), passing the church on the right, and soon after the end of the houses turn right along a hedge-lined track (G) and follow it down to a parking area. Go through a metal kissing-gate and continue across the open grassy area of the Warren down to the river (H).

Turn right to follow a path beside the river – the Bailey Walk, named after Sir Joseph Bailey, lord of the manor, who laid it out in 1884. It is an attractive and popular riverside ramble which makes a pleasant finale to the walk. Initially the path crosses meadows and later it continues through woodland that slopes steeply to the river, with plenty of seats on which to pause and enjoy the fine views across the Wye. At Hay Bridge turn right up to the road, turn left into the town and take the first road on the right to make your way through the town centre back to the start.

11 Wench Ford, Danby Lodge and Blackpool Bridge

Start:	Forestry Commission car park and picnic area at Wench Ford
Distance:	5 miles (8 km)
Approximate time:	2½ hours
Parking:	Wench Ford car park
Refreshments:	None
Ordnance Survey maps:	Landranger 162 (Gloucester & Forest of Dean) and Outdoor Leisure 14 (Wye Valley & Forest of Dean)

General description *From an exceptionally attractive picnic site the walk climbs steeply through thick woodland onto a ridge from which the views across the Forest of Dean are magnificent. Most of this fairly energetic walk is through lovely broad-leaved woodland and a number of different aspects of the forest's heritage can be appreciated – deciduous and conifer forest, part of a* disused railway, one of the surviving forest lodges, a coal mine and a short stretch of ancient road.

Wench Ford is an outstandingly attractive spot: picnic tables are set in grassy glades and amidst fine old oaks beside the babbling waters of Blackpool Brook. The walk starts opposite the toilet block. Go down steps at a 'Start of Forest Trail' sign and bear left towards Blackpool Brook. Do not cross the footbridge but turn left to walk beside the brook as far as a track; here turn right over the brook and continue up to the road a few yards ahead (**A**).

Cross over, turn right for a few yards and then turn left along a grassy path. Almost immediately bear right at a fork along an uphill path, soon meeting the red-waymarked posts of a forest trail which are followed for a large part of the walk. On reaching a broad, undulating track (**B**) turn right along it – it curves left and then right – and follow it for ¼ mile (0·5 km), keeping a sharp lookout for a red-waymarked post to the left of it just in front of a frequently dried-up pond. Here leave the track to continue along a path to the left of and initially running parallel to it, but soon turning sharply to the left and heading uphill. Cross over a track and bear left, continuing more steeply uphill to reach another path (**C**).

Here the main route turns sharply to the right along this path but a brief detour to the left – following the red waymarks in a clockwise direction around the boundary wall of Danby Lodge to rejoin the route a short distance ahead – enables you to see two differing aspects of the forest's history: the lodge and a small coal mine. Danby Lodge, now a private residence, was one of six new lodges built in the 1670s to house forest officials. The coal mine passed on this short circuit is one of the few 'free mines' still operating in the forest. A 'free miner' is allowed to mine coal completely independently and to qualify for this right he has to be born within the Hundred of St Briavels (roughly corresponding to the forest) and to have worked in a mine for not less than a year and a day.

On rejoining the main route continue along the path which soon passes the viewpoint of the Jesus Rock, an outcrop of quartz conglomerate, on the right. As this is a ridge path the views to the right over the dense unbroken forest are constantly magnificent, making the climb eminently worthwhile. The path later curves to the left and descends to a broad forest track; cross this and bear right along a winding downhill path, turning left to keep above and parallel to a road on the right. At a red waymark turn right to head downhill, finally descending to reach the road (**D**).

SCALE 1:25 000 or 2½ INCHES to 1 MILE

0   1 Kilometre

0   ½ mile

The scattered oaks and grassy glades at Wench Ford

Cross over, climb a stile and footbridge opposite and turn right along a narrow path that runs parallel to both Blackpool Brook and the road on the right. Soon the path broadens out, starts to climb and bears left away from the brook. Cross a track and keep ahead, turning right at a red waymark and continuing uphill to join a broad track. Keep ahead along this track, which soon flattens out; as this is another ridge walk there are more superb views to the right. Later the track starts to descend. Climb a stile and, ignoring a red waymark, turn to the right — this is where the route leaves the forest trail. Continue along the track for another ½ mile (0·75 km), eventually curving to the right past a forestry barrier to reach a road.

Cross over, continue along the tarmac track opposite for about 50 yards (46 m) to a crossroads and then turn right (**E**) along a stony track for just under ½ mile (0·75 km). After heading steadily uphill the track flattens out; at this point turn right (**F**) along a grassy track to continue through a particularly

attractive area of traditional forest landscape. Keep ahead at a crossroads and later the track curves to the right and heads gently downhill to a T-junction. Here turn right down to the road, turning sharp left (**G**) along it for the short distance to Blackpool Bridge. This is a delightful spot where the bridge crosses the brook and beyond it, on the right, is a short section of exposed early paved and curved road, certainly of great antiquity and thought likely to be Roman. It was part of the Dean Road, an ancient routeway through the forest.

Continue along the road under a disused railway bridge and turn left to re-enter Wench Ford picnic site, heading slightly uphill to follow the track of the old Central railway, one of many that were constructed in the Forest of Dean during the nineteenth century, mainly to carry coal. It was closed in 1962.

The track leads back to the start, but a pleasant alternative is to descend to the brook and follow a parallel path alongside it.

12 Skenfrith and Garway

Ordnance Survey maps: Landranger 161 (Abergavenny & the Black Mountains) and Pathfinder 1064, SO 42/52 (Ross-on-Wye (West))

Start: Skenfrith

Distance: 5½ miles (8·75 km)

Approximate time: 3 hours

Parking: Parking area in front of Skenfrith Castle

Refreshments: Pub and tea rooms at Skenfrith, pub at Garway

General description Most of this route is along quiet, narrow, roughish country lanes, little more than farm tracks, amidst the beautiful scenery of the Monnow valley on the border between Wales and England. Nowadays this border country is so quiet and peaceful that it is difficult to envisage it as the

Skenfrith Castle – one of the 'Trilateral' fortresses of the Monnow valley

bloody battleground that it was in the early Middle Ages, though Skenfrith Castle and the two highly distinctive border churches at Skenfrith and Garway are reminders. The ascent from Skenfrith to the hilltop village of Garway is quite steep and the views over the valley are superb.

SCALE 1:25 000 or 2½ INCHES to 1 MILE

Skenfrith is a typical border village with a border castle and a border church. The castle is one of the 'Trilateral' castles built by Hubert de Burgh in the thirteenth century to protect the Monnow valley. It is a simple but striking building, comprising a curtain wall and four rounded towers, within which are the remains of a rare circular keep. The tiny village comprises little more than a row of cottages along the lane beside the castle which leads to Skenfrith's other gem: the thirteenth-century church, contemporary with the castle and built by the same man. It is an interesting and sturdy-looking building with thick walls and a massive low tower capped by a wooden belfry that doubled up as a dovecote. The tower gives the church an almost fortress-like appearance and was in fact used as a refuge by villagers during times of trouble.

Start by walking up to the main road, turn left and turn left again over the River Monnow. Take the first turning on the left (**A**), at a notice saying 'Narrow Lane Unsuitable for Long Vehicles', and follow this winding lane for 1½ miles (2·5 km) up to Garway. In width, surface and usage the lane is little more than a farm track — it soon joins the river on the left, keeps below steep woodland on the right, heads uphill, temporarily descends and then climbs again, giving fine views over the Monnow valley, to reach the scattered, widely spaced, hilltop village of Garway.

Just before reaching the village turn right (**B**) at a 'Church Way' sign along a track to the church. Like the church at Skenfrith this is a typical Norman border church with a fortress feel about it and a solid-looking square tower that could serve as a place of refuge. It is unusual both in its history and appearance. Originally it was one of only six churches in England built by the Knights Templars, on land given to the Order by Henry II in the twelfth century. On the dissolution of that Order in 1408 it passed to their rivals, the Knights Hospitallers. Its appearance is unusual in that the tower is built at an angle to the main body of the church; originally it was detached and it only became joined to the rest of the church in the seventeenth century. The interior is dominated by the superb Norman chancel arch.

Pass through the churchyard, keeping to the left of the church, go through a metal kissing-gate and head diagonally uphill across

a cultivated field to go through another kissing-gate in the far corner. Turn right along the road through the village and just after passing the Garway Inn on the left turn right (**C**), along the lane signposted to Skenfrith and Abergavenny, across the relatively small but open expanse of Garway Common, from which there are fine views all around. Follow this lane around left- and right-hand bends, continue by the right-hand edge of Newhouse Wood to a junction and turn right (**D**) along a quiet, narrow lane for ¼ mile (0·5 km), heading downhill.

At the bottom of a dip look out for a stile on the left (**E**), climb it and head downhill along the right-hand edge of a field, by a wire fence and line of trees on the right. Climb a stile at the bottom end of the field and turn left along the lane, rejoining the outward route. Retrace your steps to Skenfrith and towards the end there are attractive views to the right of both the castle and church across the meadows bordering the Monnow.

13 Hereford and Dinedor Hill

Start·	Hereford
Distance:	6½ miles (10·5 km)
Approximate time:	3 hours
Parking:	Hereford
Refreshments:	Pubs, restaurants and cafés at Hereford, Wye Inn at Lower Bullingham
Ordnance Survey maps:	Landranger 149 (Hereford & Leominster) and Pathfinder 1040, SO 43/53 (Hereford (South) & area)

General description *Dinedor Hill is the prominent hill (600 feet (183 m)) lying to the south-east of Hereford and both its slopes and summit provide extensive views over the surrounding countryside. It is an easy hill to climb, and in addition to the views its beech-clad summit is a delight in its own right. The walk starts in the centre of Hereford, which involves a small amount of suburban road walking, but this is more than compensated for by a delightful walk across Bishop's Meadow by the banks of the placid River Wye and, on the return leg, superb views of Hereford Cathedral.*

Substantial sections of Hereford's medieval walls survive, a reminder of its long history as an important border stronghold, but of its once powerful castle nothing remains, the site now occupied by colourful ornamental gardens. Going back even further is Hereford's history as an ecclesiastical centre, the diocese being one of the oldest in England, founded in 676. The imposing cathedral lies on the north bank of the Wye, its exterior dominated by the massive, fourteenth-century central tower which rises nobly above the river and is visible from many of the surrounding higher points. The present building was begun by the first Norman bishop in the late eleventh century and is a mixture of Norman and Gothic styles, noted for its fine twelfth-century nave, thirteenth-century east end and north transept, as well as the central tower. There was once another tower above the west front but this collapsed in 1786, causing a major reconstruction of the west front; there was a further reconstruction at the beginning of the present century. Two of the cathedral's greatest treasures are the chained library and the Mappa Mundi

(map of the world), one of the greatest surviving examples of the skill of medieval cartographers.

Start at Wye Bridge and take the tree lined, tarmac path on the south side of the river across the pleasant open area of park and playing fields known as Bishop's Meadow, donated to the people of the city by a former bishop of Hereford. Pass Victoria Bridge, a suspension footbridge, and at the end of the meadow continue along the riverside path by the backs of houses, soon turning right (**A**) up to a road. Keep ahead along the road for a few yards, take the first turning on the left (Putson Avenue) and walk through suburban housing, turning right at a T-junction and continuing to the main road.

Turn left and soon after passing the Wye Inn on the left turn right along Lower Bullingham Lane (**B**). Follow this lane for nearly ¾ mile (1·25 km), passing under a railway bridge and climbing gently to a road junction (**C**). Cross over and climb a stile, at a footpath sign, to follow a path across a field, descending to cross a brook and climbing up the other side towards farm buildings. Pass through the farm buildings and continue along the lane ahead into the hamlet of Bullinghope, dominated by its fine Victorian church that was built to replace a medieval predecessor.

Just before reaching a black and white house turn left (**D**) over a stile, by a footpath sign, along a clear, broad track which heads downhill across fields. In front is a good view of Dinedor Hill. The track bears right, crosses a brook and then bears left to continue across fields, by the brook on the left. The track has now become a narrower path. Climb a stile and keep ahead, by a hedge and orchard on the left, to climb another stile onto a road. Turn left for a few yards to a junction (**E**), cross over, climb a stile by a footpath sign and head downhill along a faint path, keeping roughly parallel to a hedge on the left. Descend to cross a footbridge over a brook, climb a stile and continue along a much clearer path which heads uphill along the left-hand edge of a field, by a hedge on the left, to a stile. Climb it, bear left for a few yards along a track and then bear right along a narrow but clear path that heads steeply uphill through woodland, keeping ahead at a fork to join a narrow lane. Turn left and, in front of a house, follow the lane as it bends to the right (**F**) and continues up to the top of Dinedor Hill, reached by a short flight of steps. The views from the summit, which is crowned by superb old beeches on the site of an Iron Age fort which is now a popular picnic area, are both extensive and magnificent: northwards towards Hereford and southwards over the gently rolling, wooded country of the Wye Valley.

0 200 400 600 800m 1 Kilometres

0 200 400 600 800 1000 yds Miles 1

SCALE 1:25 000 or 2½ INCHES to 1 MILE

Retrace your steps downhill to where the lane bends to the left (**F**) and turn right along a track. Follow this for just over ½ mile (0·75 km) — with lovely views to the left over Hereford with the cathedral tower standing out — descending gently, passing several cottages and later keeping along the edge of woodland on the right. At a T-junction in front of houses turn left (**G**) along a tarmac lane for ¾ mile (1·25 km), going

under a railway bridge and continuing past farms and houses to a T-junction, here rejoining Lower Bullingham Lane.

Turn right for a few yards to the main road (**B**) and turn left to retrace the outward route — via Putson Avenue, along the riverside path and across Bishop's Meadow — back to the centre of Hereford: a most attractive and relaxing finale by the river with grand views of the cathedral tower ahead.

14 Ruardean and Astonbridgehill Inclosure

Refreshments:	Pub at Brierley, pub at Horsley Green
Ordnance Survey maps:	Landranger 162 (Gloucester & Forest of Dean) and Outdoor Leisure 14 (Wye Valley & Forest of Dean)

Start: Forestry Commission car park at Cannop Valley, on B4234 just to south of its junction with A4136 Monmouth-Gloucester road

Distance: 6 miles (9·5 km)

Approximate time: 3 hours

Parking: Cannop Valley car park

General description *Fifty years ago a writer described the top of Ruardean Hill as 'a bare and desolate spot, disfigured by rough wasteland, vast cinder heaps and ugly cottages'. Nowadays all that has changed, and much of this walk is through what is often referred to as post-industrial landscape, although it still reveals something of the now largely vanished industrial flavour of the*

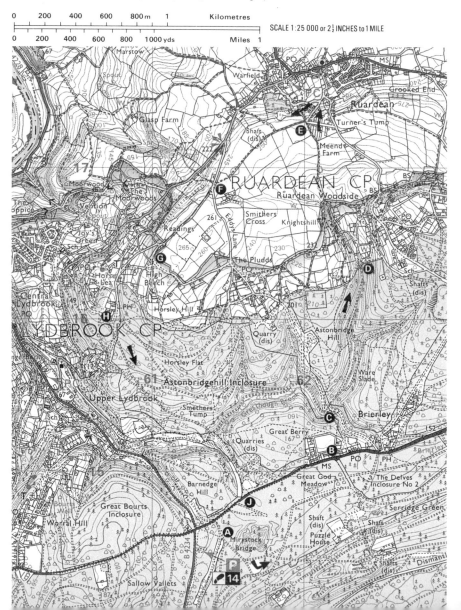

SCALE 1:25 000 or 2½ INCHES to 1 MILE

Forest of Dean, passing by abandoned mines and quarries, a former colliery village and disused railway lines. The walk also includes some splendid woodland, a fine medieval church and outstanding views, especially from the 932-foot- (284 m) high Ruardean Hill which overlooks a magnificent and extensive panorama across the Wye Valley to the Malverns and Black Mountains on the horizon.

With your back to the road follow the path in front, waymarked with green-topped posts, a short distance to a junction of paths and tracks. Do not follow the green-waymarked trail fully to the right but bear right over Mirystock Bridge (**A**), one of the many disused railway bridges in the forest, and continue along a pleasant path to a crossroads. Turn left along a track to a T-junction and here bear left along another 'track. On the hill ahead the houses of Lydbrook can be seen and to the right are old overgrown mining shafts. Climb a stile beside a gate and keep ahead, later turning right and continuing to another stile. Climb that, keep ahead a few yards to a T-junction and turn left along a tarmac track to a road (**B**).

Turn right along the road through Brierley and just before reaching the Swan Inn turn sharp left along the first of two turnings to the left — the one signposted 'The Pludds'. Follow a lane for ¼ mile (0·5 km) into a lovely steep-sided wooded valley as far as a small bridge over Greathough Brook just before a sharp right-hand bend. Here turn right (**C**), passing a forestry barrier, along a broad track by the brook on the right. Soon the track bears right to cross the brook but you keep ahead along a narrow and most attractive shady path which climbs gently and eventually emerges from the trees. Continue between bracken to reach a lane at a sharp bend (**D**).

Continue uphill along the left-hand arm of the lane. Across the valley to the right is the former colliery settlement of Ruardean Woodside but the junction is the only obvious evidence of its former mining activities. Where the lane ends a public footpath sign directs you to a stile ahead. Climb it, walk along the right-hand edge of a field, by a wire fence and hedge on the right, climb another stile and continue, now along the left-hand edge of a field with a hedge on the left. Keep to the left of a waste-tip and continue to a stone stile. The open countryside here makes a pleasant contrast to the earlier, and later, confines of the forest. Climb the stile and continue across Ruardean Hill along a narrow path that squeezes between hedges and fences on both sides to reach a lane (**E**). From this high point on the northern edge of the Forest of

Dean there stretches ahead a magnificent view over the Wye Valley, with Ruardean village and the tower and spire of its church in the foreground, the Malvern Hills on the right-hand horizon and the Black Mountains on the horizon to the left.

If you wish to visit Ruardean turn half-right and head down Kingsway Lane. The village has pubs and an interesting church of Norman origin which is chiefly noted for its fine fourteenth-century spire. Return to (**E**) by the same route.

The main route continues by turning left, at a public footpath sign, along a pleasant hedge-enclosed path. Climb a stile and keep along the right-hand edge of a field, by a hedge and wire fence on the right. From here the contrasting views — to the right over the gentle and pastoral Wye Valley and to the left over the thickly wooded and formerly industrial forest — make this part of the walk seem almost like a frontier. About halfway along the field turn right over a stile, now continuing along the left-hand edge of a field. Climb a stile and walk across the corner of a field to climb another stile onto a road (**F**) and ahead is another magnificent view across the Wye Valley to the line of the Black Mountains.

Turn left for a few yards and then bear right along a tree-lined track to reach another road at a bend. Bear slightly left along the road to where it bends to the left, just past the last of the houses, here bearing slightly right (**G**) along a grassy downhill track. Cross another track and keep ahead — the track now narrows to a path — into the woodlands of Astonbridgehill Inclosure. On entering the woodland bear slightly right to follow a path quite steeply downhill onto a lane at Horsley Green opposite the Masons Arms.

Turn left down the lane to where it bends sharply to the right and here continue straight ahead along a narrow path (**H**). Keep ahead at a crossroads of paths and shortly afterwards bear slightly left to continue through the forest along what is now a broad path. This is one of the finest sections of the walk. Keep more or less in a straight line, heading downhill all the while through beautiful woodland, later descending quite steeply to reach a T-junction of paths. Bear left, then immediately turn right to continue to a junction and here bear right to follow a path through an area of disused quarries, now completely overgrown, heading uphill. Cross a track, continue uphill and then bear right along a narrow path to the Gloucester – Monmouth road (**J**).

Turn right, heading downhill, and just before a signpost and crossroads ahead turn left along a path that leads to the junction by Mirystock Bridge (**A**). Here turn right for the short distance back to the starting point.

15 Tidenham Chase and Wintour's Leap

Start:	Forestry Commission car park and picnic area at Tidenham
Distance:	7 miles (11·25 km)
Approximate time:	3½ hours
Parking:	Tidenham car park
Refreshments:	None
Ordnance Survey maps:	Landranger 162 (Gloucester & Forest of Dean) and Outdoor Leisure 14 (Wye Valley & Forest of Dean)

General description *Tidenham Chase is a southern outlier of the Forest of Dean and nowadays chiefly comprises a mixture of open heathland and conifer plantations. It occupies a triangular-shaped undulating plateau between the Severn estuary and the Wye Valley, and from this high, open ground there are extensive views across both rivers, extending in an arc from the western slopes of the Cotswolds to the wooded hills of Gwent. After descending from the chase to the village of Tidenham, the route proceeds via the magnificent viewpoint of Wintour's Leap before returning along a well-wooded section of Offa's Dyke Path high above the eastern side of the Wye Valley. On the first part of the walk, before joining Offa's Dyke Path, route-finding can present something of a challenge − there are some invisible, overgrown and uneven paths. But persevere and follow the map and directions carefully, because this splendid walk more than compensates for some minor navigational difficulties.*

From the car park start by crossing the road and going through a metal kissing-gate on the opposite side. Walk along a grassy path, bearing right and continuing between bracken. At a crossroads of paths turn right along a broad path and after 50 yards (46 m) bear left along a narrower path, shortly reaching a large, open area of grass, heather and bracken, fringed by trees and with superb views over the Severn estuary − a delightful spot. Continue in a straight line across this open area; there is no obvious path but head in a southerly direction towards the trees in front, using as a landmark the roof of a house that can be seen among them. On reaching the trees look out for a stile onto a lane.

Turn left along this narrow lane, immediately passing the house on the right whose roof formed a landmark. About 50 yards (46 m) before the lane curves to the left turn right (**A**), passing a forestry barrier, along a track that heads across rough open country, part of which is an area of felled woodland. Take the right-hand track at the first fork and keep ahead at the next fork to a crossroads. To the left is a stone monument on which the dates suggest that it commemorates Queen Victoria's Diamond Jubilee.

At the crossroads continue along a now narrower path towards the edge of the woodland in front, and at a stile another path comes in from the right. Climb the stile and keep ahead through a mixture of bracken, brambles, thorns and gorse to reach open grassland, here bearing right − there is no obvious path − and making towards a hedge on the right. Look out for a stile in the bottom right-hand corner of the field, climb it − there is a superb view from here of the Severn estuary, Severn Bridge and the houses on the edge of Chepstow − and keep ahead to another one. Climb that and continue along a now discernible path, by a hedge and line of trees on the left, to climb yet another stile. Continue by the right-hand edge of a field, climb a stile and head downhill along a pleasant, shady path to join a lane at a junction (**B**); to the right is a large house.

Take the right-hand one of the two parallel lanes ahead, signposted Tidenham, and follow it for ¾ mile (1·25 km), eventually curving left into the now predominantly modern residential village of Tidenham. Continue through the village, following the lane around a right-hand curve, and at a sharp left-hand bend (**C**) keep ahead along a track enclosed by high walls to Tidenham's delightful medieval church, which has an imposing tower and a fine position overlooking fields that sweep down to the broad expanses of the Severn.

Go through the churchyard, pass through the lych-gate at the far end, turn right over a stone stile and walk along a narrow path, after a few yards turning right again over another stile. Take note here of the quarry warning notice. Continue along a broad grassy path, by a wire fence, hedge and woodland on the left, later passing the boundary wall of a large ruined building on the right. The path curves left to a stile; climb it, continue past a barn on the right and turn right around the end of it to climb another stile. Continue along a straight grassy path, between the edge of a conifer plantation on the right and quarry workings on the left, turn sharp left, keep ahead to climb a stile on the right and continue for a few yards to reach a narrow lane.

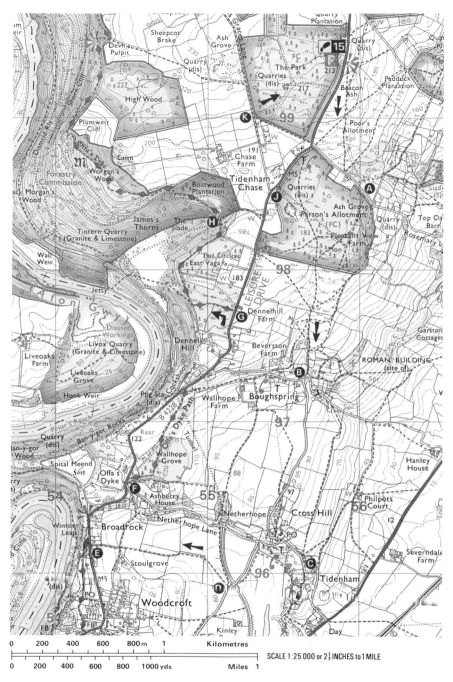

| 0 | 200 | 400 | 600 | 800 m | 1 | Kilometres |

| 0 | 200 | 400 | 600 | 800 | 1000 yds | Miles | 1 |

SCALE 1:25 000 or 2½ INCHES to 1 MILE

Turn left, cross a bridge over a disused railway and shortly afterwards turn right (**D**) over a stile beside a metal gate to follow a track across the middle of a field. Bear slightly left at the end of the field to pass through a metal gate and on along a broad, stony track. Where the track ends continue along a path that keeps by the right-hand edge of a field, by a hedge on the right, to a stile; climb it and continue along the right-hand edge of the next field, still with the hedge on the right. After the hedge ends keep ahead towards the houses in front, and just before entering the last field before those houses turn left and then immediately right to follow a rough and overgrown path along the

43

The magnificent viewpoint of Wintour's Leap – passed on walks 8 and 15

right-hand edge of a field. Go through a kissing-gate and continue along the narrow, uneven and overgrown path between houses up to the main road at Broadrock (**E**).

Turn right and soon, where the road bends to the right, you can enjoy on the left one of the finest of many fine viewpoints over the Wye – the superb view from Wintour's Leap over the great bend in the river to the wooded Wynd Cliff beyond. The viewpoint gets its name from Sir John Wintour, a Royalist supporter, who is alleged to have jumped from this spot while escaping from Parliamentary forces in 1642; in view of the height it is a highly unlikely story.

Keep along the road as far as a footpath sign to Monmouth and the distinctive Offa's Dyke Path acorn symbol, where you turn right (**F**) over a stone stile and along a path by a wire fence, hedge and woodland on the right.

Climb a stile to enter the woodland and keep along the edge of it, turning right at a waymark and continuing along its right-hand edge to climb another stile. Emerging from the wood keep along the right-hand edge of a field, by a hedge on the right, and continue

over three stiles in fairly quick succession to rejoin the road.

Turn right along the road for ½ mile (0·75 km) and at the next Offa's Dyke Path sign to Monmouth turn left (**G**) over a stile to walk along a pleasant wooded path. Climb the next stile and then the path turns to the right and continues through a most beautiful stretch of woodland, following a particularly well-preserved section of Offa's Dyke and with tantalising glimpses through the trees on the left of the Wye far below. Follow waymarks down a long flight of steps, descending to a broad forest track, and turn right (**H**) to follow the track uphill, passing through a metal gate and on to rejoin the road once more.

Turn left, soon bearing left (**J**) along a lane – Miss Grace's Lane – which runs in a straight line. At the point where this tarmac lane degenerates into a rough track turn right (**K**) through a gate, at a yellow arrow and Tidenham car park waymark, and walk along a grassy track through the conifer plantations of the Park, part of the Forestry Commission's Tidenham Chase, following it back to the starting point.

16 Goodrich Castle

Start:	Goodrich Castle car park and picnic area
Distance:	8½ miles (13·5 km)
Approximate time:	4 hours
Parking:	Goodrich Castle car park
Refreshments:	Pub at Goodrich, light snacks at Goodrich Castle picnic area
Ordnance Survey maps:	Landranger 162 (Gloucester & Forest of Dean) and Outdoor Leisure 14 (Wye Valley & Forest of Dean)

General description *Between Ross-on-Wye and Monmouth the River Wye makes a whole series of great loops. Goodrich Castle occupies the neck of one of these and this route starts from the castle and follows the loop around, passing below Coldwell Rocks and the great cliff of Symonds Yat, before returning to Goodrich. Such is the extent of the loop that all but the final mile (1·5 km) of this 8½-mile (13·5 km) walk hugs the river. It passes through some lovely riverside scenery – meadows, arable fields, woods and steep cliffs – and as most of it follows the Wye Valley Walk it is well waymarked. The spectacular castle ruins, which can be explored either at the beginning or the end, are an additional bonus.*

Refer to map overleaf.

Hereford and Worcester County Council have created a large car park and attractive picnic site just below Goodrich Castle and the ruins are reached by following a path northwards from the car park – a distance of about ¼ mile (0·5 km). The red sandstone walls and towers look most striking and dramatic standing high above the Wye Valley. The original small twelfth-century keep in the middle of the castle buildings was made virtually redundant by an extensive rebuilding in the late thirteenth and fourteenth centuries and is now dwarfed by the later massive curtain walls, rounded corner towers, strong gatehouse and semi-circular barbican. These, together with the moat and the castle's elevated defensive position, give an impression of apparent impregnability – in fact the castle was only captured once in its long history, by Parliamentary forces during the Civil War.

From the car park walk back along the drive down to a crossroads (**A**), bear slightly left, passing a school on the right, and at the next junction turn sharp left along a road

signposted to Ross-on-Wye and Coleford. Pass under a bridge and head down to the river; just before reaching the river you pass farm buildings on the left that incorporate part of the medieval Flanesford Priory.

In front of the river bridge turn right (**B**) over a stile, at a Wye Valley Walk sign, and go down steps to follow a riverside path. To the right is the only view of Goodrich Castle on the entire walk. Keep along this right bank of the river for the next 3¼ miles (5·25 km), following it around the great loop and over several stiles. At first the path, which is narrow at times, goes across meadows, then it undulates below steep, thickly wooded banks on the right. It then crosses more pleasant riverside meadows, continues along the edge of fields and finally crosses more meadows to reach Welsh Bicknor, which comprises little more than a small Victorian church and the youth hostel.

Continue by the river, following Wye Valley Walk signs and ignoring a footpath sign to the right to Goodrich, to pass through more woodland and then turn left over a disused railway bridge (**C**). On the other side of the river turn left down some steps, turn left again to pass under the bridge and continue along the left bank of the Wye, over several stiles and through a number of gates – initially you keep along the edge of fields, then follow a disused railway track below thickly wooded banks on the left, and continue across a most attractive area of sloping meadowland. After a turn to the right, walk through the woods at the base of the almost perpendicular Symonds Yat Rock. Head slightly uphill to reach the second of two signs pointing to Yat Rock on the left and follow Wye Valley Walk signs to the right, down a flight of steps and along a narrow, downhill, twisting, wooded path to continue by the river. Climb gently again to a Wye Valley Walk waymark to the left of a large rock and bear right (**D**), here leaving the Wye Valley Walk, along a path which continues to wind between trees for a short distance before emerging from them.

Continue along the edge of fields that border the Wye, with the spire of Goodrich church prominent ahead. What is initially a superb, broad, grassy path later degenerates into a narrow, overgrown, and at times difficult, field-edge path before reaching the road by Huntsham Bridge (**E**). Turn right over the bridge, keep ahead to a T-junction and turn right (**F**) along the road signposted to Ross-on-Wye, Coleford and Goodrich, heading gently uphill. Keep along the road for ¾ mile (1·25 km), passing Goodrich's large thirteenth- and fourteenth-century church on the hill to the left, and at the crossroads (**A**) bear right along the drive back to Goodrich Castle picnic area.

17 Ross-on-Wye and Penyard Hill

Start:	Ross-on-Wye
Distance:	7 ½ miles (12 km)
Approximate time:	4 hours
Parking:	Ross-on-Wye
Refreshments:	Pubs, restaurants and cafés at Ross-on-Wye, pub at Weston under Penyard
Ordnance Survey maps:	Landranger 162 (Gloucester & Forest of Dean), Pathfinders 1064, SO 42/52 (Ross-on-Wye (West)) and 1065, SO 62/72 (Ross-on-Wye (East))

General description *Penyard Hill is the prominent, thickly wooded hill that lies immediately to the south-east of Ross-on-Wye and was once a chase belonging to the Bishops of Hereford. From it, especially the higher slopes, there are open and expansive views over the Wye Valley towards the Black Mountains of South Wales and, nearer, the northern edge of the Forest of Dean. Starting in the centre of Ross, the route leads by field paths and quiet lanes to the village of Weston under Penyard and continues over Penyard Hill, a relatively modest climb, before dropping back into Ross.*

Refer to map overleaf.

From a distance few small towns look as appealing as Ross-on-Wye, especially when viewed from the riverside meadows. Its

Ross-on-Wye occupies a splendid site above the river

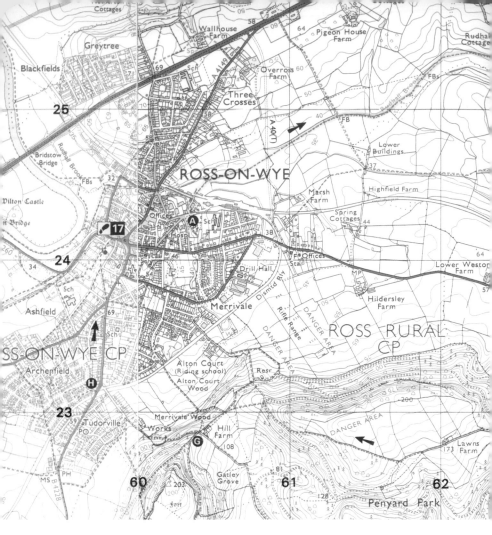

houses rise harmoniously in a series of terraces above the river, with the tower and spire of the medieval church towering above them and the whole idyllic scene backed by the wooded slopes of Penyard Hill. Closer acquaintance does nothing to diminish its appeal. Dignified old houses line its streets, it has a bustling and cheerful atmosphere as befits a market town, and there are plenty of hotels, restaurants, pubs and cafés to cater for visitors. The church is a large, handsome town church, dating from the late thirteenth century and noted for its soaring, elegant fourteenth-century spire, a conspicuous landmark for miles around. In the centre of the town at a meeting of roads stands the seventeenth-century red-sandstone Market House.

From the Market House head eastwards along the B4260 and turn half-left (not along Henry Street but along Cantilupe Road to its right), passing the library on the left. At the bottom of the road turn right for a few yards and then turn left, by the side of a supermarket car park on the left, along a broad track (**A**) – there is a public footpath sign further on. Pass between the supports of a former railway bridge, continue across an industrial estate, and on along a wide path between wire fences to go through a metal gate. At a yellow waymark a few yards ahead bear right over a stile.

Walk in a straight line across a field – there is no obvious path – aiming for a point about halfway along the wooden fence at the far end of the field where there is a stile. Climb it, go up some steps, cross a road, go down steps on the other side, turn left for a few yards and then turn right over a stile. Continue across a field, heading towards the wire fence, line of trees and brook on the left, then keep along the left-hand edge of a series of fields, by the brook on the left all the while, climbing a succession of stiles. Parts of this path may be muddy and overgrown but as compensation there are pleasant, open views

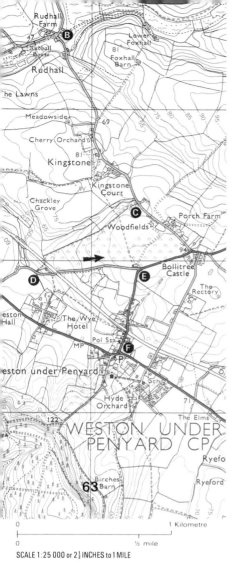

SCALE 1:25 000 or 2½ INCHES to 1 MILE

edge of an orchard, by a wire fence and line of trees now on the right. From here there are fine views over Ross and across the Wye Valley to the Black Mountains on the horizon. At the end of the orchard follow the edge of it round to the left for a few yards to a stile, climb over and head downhill across a field to a metal gate and footpath sign. Go through onto a lane (**D**), turn left and at the first junction, signposted to Weston under Penyard and Ross-on-Wye, turn right (**E**) to follow the road into the village of Weston under Penyard, the tower of its church standing out prominently against the wooded slopes of Penyard Hill.

At the crossroads in the village turn right (**F**) for a few yards and then turn left along an uphill lane, passing the church on the left; the lane later degenerates into a rough, hedge-lined track which climbs gently up the lower slopes of Penyard Hill. On entering woodland the track forks — take the right-hand fork and continue through the trees to the next fork, here turning sharp left uphill. At a T-junction turn right along a track, climbing a stile beside a gate on the edge of woodland and continuing to Lawns Farm. From this elevated position there are superb views to the left over the valley and the edge of the Forest of Dean. Follow the track past the farm, go through a metal gate and continue along the right-hand edge of a field, by a hedge on the right, turning right over a stile by another metal gate. Just before reaching the stile, the few crumbling walls that can be seen on the edge of the trees below are all that remain of the medieval Penyard Castle.

Continue along a narrow path by the right-hand edge of the woodlands of Penyard Park. The path squeezes between the trees on the left and a wire fence on the right, eventually bearing slightly left to enter the woods and heading down to join a broad track. Turn right along this track and just before it curves to the right on the edge of the woodland turn left down to a stile. Climb it and continue gently downhill straight across a field, making for a gap between two belts of woodland and bearing left to a stile, metal gate and Wye Valley Walk sign immediately. Climb the stile and bear left along a wooded path to emerge at a crossroads of tracks and paths just to the right of Hill Farm (**G**).

Turn right along a broad, downhill track lined by tall trees and where the track becomes a tarmac road continue between modern houses down to a main road (**H**). Turn right along the road as far as a small recreation ground on the left and bear left onto the tarmac path that crosses it, heading directly for the spire of Ross church. Continue through a car park and bear right along Church Street, passing to the right of the church, to return to the starting point.

all around. After crossing a footbridge over the brook go through a metal gate, continue along the edge of the next field, bear left to a stile in it immediately and bear to the right, making for the hedge in front. Here bear right again to join a track and at the end of the field go through the right-hand one of two metal gates and continue along a track, between a hedge on the left and wall on the right, to join a lane.

Turn right along the lane and take the first turning on the right (**B**), signposted to Bromsash and Weston under Penyard, following this lane for ¾ mile (1·25 km). Just before a row of houses on the left turn right over a stile (**C**) at a footpath sign and walk along a track, later bearing left uphill away from the track to keep by a wire fence on the left. Turn left over a stile in that fence and immediately turn right along the right-hand

18 Monmouth and the Kymin

Start:	Monmouth
Distance:	7 miles (11·25 km)
Approximate time:	3½ hours
Parking:	Monmouth
Refreshments:	Pubs, restaurants and cafés at Monmouth, pub at Redbrook
Ordnance Survey maps:	Landranger 162 (Gloucester & Forest of Dean) and Outdoor Leisure 14 (Wye Valley & Forest of Dean)

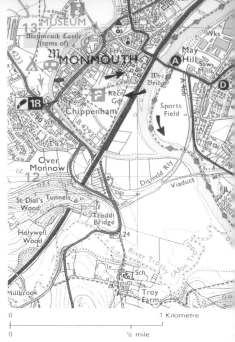

SCALE 1:25 000 or 2½ INCHES to 1 MILE

General description *This route utilises stretches of both the Wye Valley Walk and Offa's Dyke Path to make an attractive, varied but at the same time relatively undemanding circular walk between Monmouth and Redbrook. A gentle initial stroll along the banks of the River Wye is followed by a modest climb, and the return high-level route gives superb views across the valley to the Black Mountains. The scenic highlight is the magnificent viewpoint of the Kymin, which rises 800 feet (244 m) above Monmouth. From here a descent through particularly attractive woodland leads back to the town.*

The fine old town of Monmouth occupies a strategic position at the confluence of the rivers Wye and Monnow, on the border of Wales and England. In front of the eighteenth-century Shire Hall in Agincourt Square stand statues of the town's two most illustrious sons, who found fame in totally different fields and who are separated in time by nearly five centuries: Charles Rolls, co-founder of Rolls-Royce, and King Henry V, victor of the battle which gives its name to the square. Of the castle in which the latter was born little remains — stones from it were used in the construction of the seventeenth-century Great Castle House nearby. The most imposing reminder of Monmouth's former history as a great border stronghold is the unique, thirteenth-century fortified gatehouse on the bridge over the Monnow at the bottom end of the long main street.

The walk starts at this bridge. Walk away from it towards the town centre and take the first turning on the right by the cattle market, curving left by the side of a recreation ground and turning right to follow a straight tarmac path across the recreation ground between an avenue of trees. At the far end continue past a children's play area and along a path,

between a wall bordering the main road on the right and iron railings and the buildings of Monmouth School on the left, up to a crossroads. Cross over, turn right under a subway, cross the Wye Bridge and turn right, at a public footpath sign to Redbrook, to join the Wye Valley Walk (**A**).

Go through a parking area and continue along the path straight ahead, passing behind a sports pavilion and keeping along the edge of the sports field, as it curves left keeping roughly parallel with the river on the right. At the end of the sports field pass under a disused railway bridge, then a little further on under a ruined viaduct, and continue along a riverside path for the next 2 miles (3·25 km), climbing a number of stiles. At first the path is shady and tree-lined, later it crosses lovely riverside meadows, then it undulates below a steep, wooded cliff and finally it crosses more meadows parallel to the main road on the left.

Eventually you join the road; walk along it into Redbrook and take the first turning on the left (**B**), signposted to Coleford, Newland and Lydney. Head uphill and at a footpath sign to Monmouth and the familiar Offa's Dyke Path acorn symbol bear left along a track which curves to the left and ascends steadily. Climb a stile beside a metal gate, keep ahead, cross over a junction of paths and continue by a wire fence on the right. There are now lovely open views on both sides, to the left over the Wye Valley and to the right over the Forest of Dean.

Climb a stile, keep ahead — now with the wire fence on the left — to another stile,

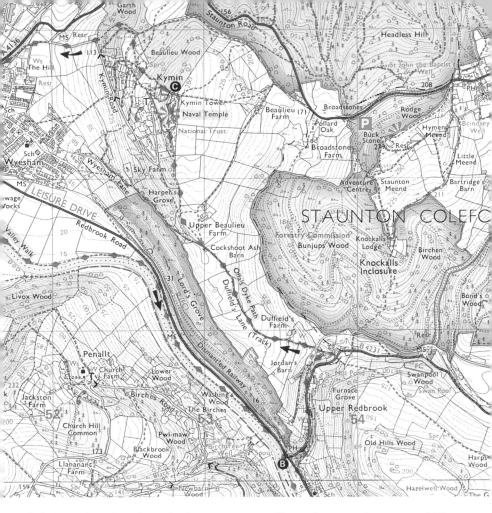

climb that and continue along what is now an enclosed track. Turn right over a stile at an Offa's Dyke Path waymark and turn left, continuing in the same direction and climbing another waymarked stile in front. Keep ahead along the top edge of the woodland on the left to a stile, climb it and continue along a path that squeezes between a wire fence on the right and the edge of the woodland. Climb another stile, continue to a metal kissing-gate in a wall, pass through that and follow a narrow, shady path to go through another metal kissing-gate into the National Trust car park at the Kymin. A short distance ahead are the two structures that crown this wooded summit. The first is the Naval Temple, built in 1800 to commemorate recent British naval triumphs and the sixteen admirals responsible for them, including Nelson who came here while on a visit to the Wye Valley in 1802. Just beyond the temple is the Round House, constructed in 1793 as a summer-house for the wealthy gentlemen of Monmouth who could eat, drink and generally make merry while enjoying the

magnificent view over the town and Wye Valley to the Black Mountains.

After passing the Round House turn left (**C**), at a footpath sign to Monmouth, and head downhill through thick woodland. Climb a stile to leave the woods and walk along a tarmac lane for a few yards before turning right over a stile and continuing downhill across a field to climb a waymarked stile ahead. Bear slightly right downhill across the next field, following marker-posts to a stile in the bottom corner. Climb it, turn left at a fork immediately in front and head gently downhill through a most attractive stretch of woodland, passing through a gate onto a lane.

Continue downhill along this lane and where it bends sharply to the right keep ahead along a track at a public footpath sign to Monmouth. Bear slightly right off this track to pass through a metal kissing-gate and continue along a wooded path, heading gently downhill to join a road (**D**). Follow the road as it curves to the right, recrossing the Wye Bridge and retracing your steps to the starting point by the Monnow Bridge.

19 Dymock and Kempley Green

Start:	Forestry Commission car park at Queen's Wood, ¼ mile (0·5 km) south of Kempley Green
Distance:	8½ miles (13·5 km)
Approximate time:	4½ hours
Parking:	Queen's Wood car park
Refreshments:	Pub at Dymock
Ordnance Survey maps:	Landranger 149 (Hereford & Leominster), Pathfinders 1065, SO 62/72 (Ross-on-Wye (East)) and 1041, SO 63/73 (Ledbury & Much Marcle)

General description *Most of this walk follows the Daffodil Way, a highly attractive and well-waymarked route through the flat terrain of the Leadon valley in north-west Gloucestershire, opened in 1988 through the initiative of the Windcross Public Paths Project. The excellent waymarking makes it easy to follow but sections are fairly tortuous and you therefore need to keep a sharp lookout for the frequent yellow arrows with black dots. The route goes across fields and meadows, passes through woodlands and orchards, and includes the interesting village of Dymock and two outstanding medieval churches. It gets its name from the wild daffodils that are such a feature of the area during spring, though they no longer grow in such profusion as in the days before the First World War when Lascelles Abercrombie, one of the band of celebrated 'Dymock Poets', wrote:*

> *From Dymock, Kempley, Newent*
>   *Bromsberrow*
> *Redmarley, all the meadowland Daffodils*
>   *seen*
> *Running in golden tides to Ryton Firs*

Queen's Wood, along with neighbouring Dymock Wood, is part of the Forestry Commission's Dymock Forest. From the car park turn left along the road to the edge of Kempley Green and at a public footpath sign by a bungalow turn right (**A**) onto a track, almost immediately turning right again between two bungalows to a stile. Here you join the Daffodil Way and from now on you need to look out for the yellow arrows with black spots.

Climb a stile and walk along the left-hand edge of a field, by a hedge and wire fence on the left, and ahead there are pleasant views across fields to Dymock Wood. Climb a stile at the bottom end of the field and, passing to the right of a barn, continue between a wire fence on the left and a line of trees on the right to a metal gate. Go through and keep in the same direction across the middle of the next field, crossing a brook and continuing to a stile on the edge of Dymock Wood. Climb it and follow a narrow but well-waymarked path through this lovely area of woodland. The end of the wood is heralded by the noise of traffic on the nearby M50 and the path joins a broad track. On reaching a lane turn right (**B**), and just before the motorway bridge turn left to follow a lane parallel to the motorway; this is the only noisy part of an otherwise very tranquil walk.

Where the lane curves to the left keep ahead through a metal gate at a public footpath sign and continue along the right-

SCALE 1:25 000 or 2½ INCHES to 1 MILE

52

hand edge of a field, by a hedge bordering the motorway on the right. From here there are fine wide views across the fields on the left to the Malverns. Continue along the right-hand edge of fields, going through two more gates before turning left away from the motorway to follow a line of trees and a brook on the right. Climb a stile, cross a farm track, climb another stile opposite and continue along the right-hand edge of a field, passing through a metal gate and then turning left along a track a few yards ahead. Go through a gate and keep ahead beside part of a disused eighteenth-century canal on the right, following the track first to the right and then to the left and continuing through a narrow belt of woodland. On reaching a T-junction of tracks turn right over a bridge, immediately turn left to climb a stile at a public footpath sign, and keep along a narrow path, still by the canal on the left. Climb another stile and continue to where the

canal ends; here cross a footbridge and keep along the right-hand edge of several fields, by a hedge and brook on the right all the time, climbing a succession of stiles.

Soon the houses and church tower of Dymock can be seen ahead. Where the hedge on the right bends to the right keep ahead to climb a stile and then continue towards the church, and the pub beside it, at first across an orchard and then along the left-hand edge of a field, finally climbing a stile into the village (**C**).

Cross the road and take the path opposite up to the lych-gate, going through into the churchyard. Dymock is a pleasant, tranquil old village dominated by its fine church which, though mainly fourteenth-century, still retains some Norman work, notably a twelfth-century south doorway. In the church there is an exhibition to the 'Dymock Poets', a gathering of some of the most talented and celebrated poets of their day

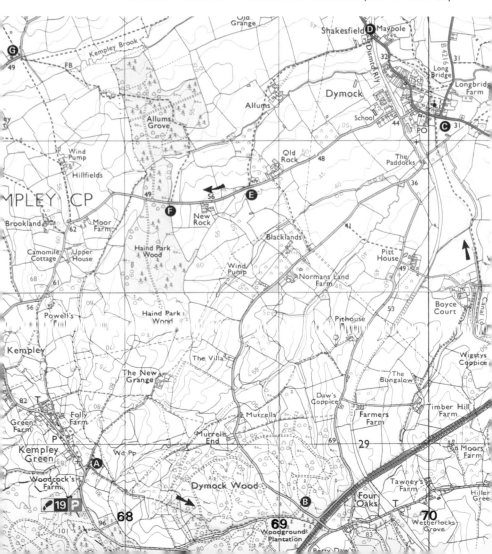

who all lived in the area in the years immediately before the First World War. The distinguished circle included Lascelles Abercrombie, Rupert Brooke, John Drinkwater, Wilfrid Gibson, Edward Thomas and Robert Frost, but the war separated its members for ever.

Pass in front of the church tower and continue along a tree-lined path to go through a kissing-gate. Bear left and head across a field, in the direction of a footpath sign, making for a hedge corner on the left. Follow the hedge and line of trees, keeping to the right of them, for about 50 yards (46 m), and where the hedge bends to the left keep ahead to cross a footbridge and continue in the same direction – there is no obvious path – across the next field, climbing a stile and turning right onto a stretch of old road. The road soon ends at a barrier and here turn left down to the new road (D), cross it and take the track ahead. Where the track bears left towards a farmhouse keep ahead, by a hedge on the right, go through a gap in the hedge in front and veer left to the end of a barn. Here pick up a clear field path, keeping to the right of farm buildings and making for a metal gate to an orchard. Walk through the orchard, bearing right and keeping by a hedge on the left, climb a stile at the far end and continue along the left-hand edge of a field to go through a metal gate onto a road (E).

Turn right along the road as far as a footpath sign, where the road enters a belt of woodland (F). Turn right over a stile and walk along the right-hand edge of the woodland, looking out for a waymarked post on the left. Here turn half-right and head diagonally across the field down to a footbridge over a brook near the far corner. Cross the footbridge and climb a stile a few yards ahead to enter woodland, turning right along a path and following it as it curves left to a stile. Turn right over the stile, then turn left along the edge of the woodland, shortly climbing another stile to re-enter the wood. Now turn left to follow the well-waymarked track through the dense conifers of Allums Grove, bearing right at the first T-junction, turning left at the next T-junction, keeping ahead at a crossroads of tracks and finally going through a metal gate to emerge from the wood.

Continue straight across a field, passing to the left of a tree-encircled pond and the scanty remains of an old farm beyond it, and at the end of the field turn right through a gap in a hedge and continue along the left-hand side of the next field. Where the hedge on the left turns sharply to the left, bear left and head across the field corner to climb a stile in a hedge. Turn right along the right-hand edge of a field, by a hedge on the right, veering left away from the hedge to cross a footbridge over Kempley Brook. Turn half-left to head diagonally across the next field, climb a stile in a wire fence, continue in the same direction – there is no visible path – climb another stile and keep ahead to climb yet another stile onto a lane (G).

Turn left for ½ mile (0·75 km), passing Kempley Old Church on the left. An English Heritage notice-board says that it was built in the late eleventh or early twelfth century and was once the parish church for Kempley, but because the village slowly migrated to higher ground two miles to the south a new church was built there in 1903, making this one redundant. It contains some of the finest early medieval wall paintings in Britain, with frescos dating back to the twelfth century, and retains a superb Norman chancel arch. The church stands in a lovely setting surrounded by fields and orchards. Continue past it and at a T-junction (H) keep straight ahead at a footpath sign, climbing a stile and continuing across a field – there is no path but follow the line of telegraph poles as landmarks. A yellow waymark on the last of these poles directs you to a line of trees ahead where you veer slightly to the right to go through a metal gate.

Now comes a rather awkward section. Follow a sometimes uneven path along the left-hand edge of a series of fields, keeping by Kempley Brook on the left all the time, climbing several stiles and following the waymarks. The field edges curve a lot, following the brook's meanderings, but eventually you climb a stile onto a lane (J). Turn left along the lane for just over ¼ mile (0·5 km) to a T-junction, turn right, in the direction signposted Upton Bishop, Linton and Ross, and after 50 yards (46 m) turn left (K) over a stile at a footpath sign. Keep by a hedge on the right as it curves right to a second stile, climb that, walk along the right-hand edge of a field, by a hedge on the right, to climb a third stile and continue to a fourth one. Climb that and head straight across the next field, making for the line of trees in front.

Here cross a footbridge over a brook and bear left across a field to join and keep by a wire fence on the right that borders the garden of a large house. Go through a metal gate, continue across the next field, go through another metal gate and on across the next field to a stile in the far left-hand corner. Climb it, and another one immediately in front, continuing by a hedge on the left. Where the hedge turns sharply to the left keep straight ahead – there is no path – to the right-hand corner of a row of gardens in front, continuing to a metal gate onto the road at Kempley Green. Turn right along the road for ¼ mile (0·5 km) to return to the starting point.

20 Newnham, Blaize Bailey and Soudley Ponds

Start:	Newnham
Distance:	8 ½ miles (13·5 km)
Approximate time:	4 ½ hours
Parking:	Newnham
Refreshments:	Pubs at Newnham, light refreshments at Dean Heritage Centre at Lower Soudley
Ordnance Survey maps:	Landranger 162 (Gloucester & Forest of Dean) and Outdoor Leisure 14 (Wye Valley & Forest of Dean)

General description *This walk combines fine woodland, open vistas and a pleasant riverside section with reminders of the Forest of Dean's industrial heritage. Starting from the banks of the broad River Severn, a climb across fields to the high wooded ground on the eastern edge of the forest is followed by a descent to the attractive man-made Soudley Ponds. The walk continues through the Soudley valley, passing the Dean Heritage Centre, and leaves the forest to cross more open country and return to the banks of the Severn for a final relaxing and scenic section along part of the Severn Way Path.*

Refer to map overleaf.

Newnham, a former shipbuilding centre and river port on the Severn, has a long, wide, sloping main street at the top end of which stands the Victorian church. In spring the grass verges are carpeted with daffodils and make a splendid sight.

The walk starts at the bottom end of the main street by the river. Walk up the street through the village, and opposite the Clock Tower, erected in 1875, turn right (**A**) along Station Road, which continues as Hyde Lane. After crossing the railway the lane curves to the right but you keep ahead along a track to a footpath sign and here turn left over a stile a few yards in front. Now turn half-right and head gently uphill in a diagonal direction across a large field – the path is rather indistinct – to a stile. Climb it and continue in the same direction, with fine views of the forest ahead and of the great bends in the Severn to the left, to climb another stile onto a road.

Turn right along the road, initially heading downhill, then going uphill and passing the

Grange Village Craft Workshops on the left. Soon after a right-hand bend and opposite a barn, turn left (**B**) through a metal gate (not the sharp left turn at a bridleway sign) to follow a gently ascending track between fields on both sides to another metal gate. Go through that, continue uphill along the right-hand edge of a field, by a hedge on the right – there is no obvious path – and just before reaching a line of trees ahead turn half-left and head diagonally uphill across the rest of the field. Pass through the widely spaced line of trees and keep to the right of a house to reach a stile and footpath sign. Climb the stile, turn left along a lane, and at the next waymark a few yards ahead bear right along a track, passing to the left of a house and following yellow waymarks into the forest.

On reaching a crossroads of tracks the main route turns right but it is worth while making a short detour to the left to the Blaize Bailey viewpoint. Turn left, then bear left off the main track beside a yellow waymarked gate to continue to the Blaize Bailey viewing platform (**C**), a magnificent viewpoint over Newnham, the great sweeping bends in the broad Severn and the line of the Cotswolds on the horizon.

Retrace your steps to the crossroads of tracks to rejoin the main route, keep ahead and after 50 yards (46 m) the track bends sharply to the left and heads downhill. Through the trees on the right are grand views of farms, fields and the thick woodlands that clothe the steep sides of the Soudley valley. This part of the track is a forest drive and cars may be encountered. Continue downhill, curving left all the while, to reach the parking area by Soudley Ponds and turn left, picking up a yellow-waymarked route again and following a track that keeps along the left-hand side of the series of small ponds and the stream that feeds them. These ponds, like all the others in the forest, are man made. It was originally thought that they were created to provide water power for Camp Mill, now the Dean Heritage Centre, but it is now believed that they were made as fish ponds in the mid-nineteenth century. This is a most pleasant stretch of the walk, enhanced by the superb, tall Douglas firs to the left.

Go through a gate onto the road and turn left (**D**), passing the Dean Heritage Centre on the right. This nineteenth-century former mill building, on the site of an earlier forge, has had a variety of uses – corn mill, leather factory and saw mill – but has now taken on a new role as a museum, telling the story of the Forest of Dean, especially its industrial history, through the ages. It contains craft workshops, an adventure playground, shop and restaurant as well as the museum.

Keep along the road as it curves to the

right above the settlement of Lower Soudley and where it turns right over a bridge keep ahead (E) along a tarmac track, passing the disused Haie Hill railway tunnel on the left, part of a line that formerly linked Cinderford with Newnham and other ports on the Severn estuary. At a public bridleway sign climb a stile beside a gate, keep to the left of the next gate and continue along a very attractive path through the Soudley valley, between a wall and woodland on the left and a wire fence on the right, with the brook below on the right. Go through a gate, pass a row of cottages on the left and bear right to cross the brook. At a junction of tracks keep straight ahead along a tarmac track between houses — later this becomes a rough track which rejoins the brook but now the brook is on the left. Just after passing another row of cottages on the right, turn sharp left over a bridge and continue along what is now a narrow, winding lane.

Keep along the lane for just over ¼ mile (0·5 km). After crossing a brook the lane curves left and heads uphill, and where it starts to curve to the right turn left through a metal gate (**F**) and follow a track across a field. Go through another metal gate — the gates are in rather poor condition on this part of the walk but should present no real difficulty — and continue across the next field, soon joining and keeping along the right-hand side of a hedge. Pass to the right of Haiebrook Farm and continue by the right-hand side of the hedge, bearing right at the end of the field and passing through a gap in the hedge in front into the next field. Now follow a discernible path between grass and fern that curves right at the end of that field and continues by the edge of a plantation on the left.

Look out for a metal gate below on the edge of this plantation, turn left to go through it and almost immediately turn right to join a track. Pass through a metal gate by a cattle-grid and keep along the track for ¾ mile (1·25 km) — it bends to the right, shortly afterwards becomes a tarmac drive, passes the elegant mansion of Oaklands Park on the right and, with fine views of the forest to the left and the River Severn ahead, continues down to the Gloucester – Chepstow road. Turn left along the road for ¼ mile (0·5 km) — there is a footpath along the right-hand side of the road — and take the first turning on the right, signposted to Bullo Pill (**G**).

Walk along the lane, pass under a railway bridge and about 50 yards (46 m) ahead turn left, at a Severn Way Path signpost, onto an overgrown path that keeps by the wall of a house on the right. At the next signpost turn right along a track, between a wall on the right and a wire fence on the left, and where it curves left keep ahead along a hedge-lined path. Climb a stile, keep ahead over another one and continue along the right-hand edge of a field bordered by trees on the right. Where the field edge curves to the left above a cliff, a gap in the trees reveals a magnificent view across the broad expanse of the River Severn, with the spire of Newnham church acting as a prominent landmark. Head across the field, keeping parallel to the wooded cliff edge on the right, to the far end and continue along a very attractive wooded track, with the river immediately below. Eventually you bear slightly left away from the river and cross a field to the main road (**H**).

Turn right uphill towards Newnham and where the road curves to the left keep ahead at a footpath sign, going through the churchyard and passing in front of the church to rejoin the main road at the top of the long, broad, sloping main street. Walk down the street back to the starting point.

21 Fownhope, Brockhampton and Capler Camp

Start:	Fownhope
Distance:	8 ½ miles (13·5 km). Shorter version 6 miles (9·5 km)
Approximate time:	4 ½ hours (3 hours for shorter version)
Parking:	Near the church at Fownhope
Refreshments:	Pub at Fownhope
Ordnance Survey maps:	Landranger 149 (Hereford & Leominster), Pathfinders 1040, SO 43/53 (Hereford (South) & area) and 1041, SO 63/73 (Ledbury & Much Marcle)

General description *A pleasant village, two highly attractive and distinctive churches, a prehistoric camp, fields and farms, woodland and riverside paths — these are the main ingredients that make up a highly interesting and varied walk through one of the most scenic parts of the Wye Valley. Much of the route follows the well-waymarked Wye Valley Walk, which is fortunate as some of the field paths are quite complicated to follow and a sharp eye needs to be kept for the yellow arrows. Although there are several uphill sections, none of these are either lengthy or particularly steep.*

Refer to map overleaf.

Fownhope is a harmonious mixture of old and new buildings situated above a particularly attractive stretch of the Wye. The fine cruciform church dates from the twelfth century and retains much of the original work, including the central tower surmounted by a later spire. By the churchyard wall are the old stocks and whipping-post.

Start by the church and take the lane to the right of it, signposted to Capler. Keep along this undulating lane, from which there are constantly fine views over the valley to the right, for 1 mile (1·5 km) to where it starts to head upwards into woodland with the river immediately below (**A**).

*At this point, those wishing to do only the shorter version of the walk can continue along the lane to rejoin the main route at (**F**) below.*

Bear right at a 'Private Road' sign along a wooded track that heads gently downhill to the river and keep along it, below steep, wooded slopes on the left, to follow a particularly lovely stretch of the Wye around a great right-hand bend. The spire that can be seen on the right is that of Ballingham church. After 1 mile (1·5 km) bear left away from the river into the trees and head steeply uphill to a lane (**B**).

Turn left along the lane, passing a group of farms and cottages, and at the second group of houses, Brinkley Hill, turn sharp right (**C**), at a Wye Valley Walk marker-post, along a grassy hedge-lined track. The track soon narrows to a rather overgrown path that continues by a wire fence on the left, and at a yellow waymark turn left along another hedge-lined track that leads down to a lane. Turn right, take the first turning on the left – this is a sharp turn – and continue down another short section of lane before turning through the first metal gate on the left (**D**).

Head straight across a field, with Brockhampton Court and the ruins of the old church visible on the hill above to the right, soon picking up a distinct path that continues through a delightful shallow valley. Go through a metal gate and continue gently uphill, bearing slightly right – the path tends to peter out here – and making for the gate ahead onto a lane (**E**). Opposite is Brockhampton's highly original new church, built at the beginning of this century to replace the medieval one recently passed. It is a curious but also pleasing and harmonious blend of traditional and modern with a thatched roof, squat and heavy-looking central tower and wooden belfry at the west end.

Turn left along the lane to a crossroads and here turn right, in the direction signposted Fownhope and Hereford, soon passing Capler Lodge on the right. From here there is a particularly outstanding view over the winding, sylvan Wye. At this point the walk is rejoined by the shorter route (F). At a Wye Valley Walk signpost bear right (those doing the shorter walk turn left) through a gate and along a wooded track which heads gently uphill. On emerging from the trees bear right over a stile and follow a narrow path diagonally across a young plantation, climbing another stile at the end of it and turning right to briefly rejoin the track. The trees on the left partially encircle the earthworks of Capler Camp on the top of Capler Hill. This Iron Age fort is nearly 600 feet (183 m) above the Wye with superb views over the valley.

The track soon curves to the left but keep ahead along a path that heads through trees to a stile. Climb it and continue along a pleasant grassy path that passes between the double ramparts of the fort. Keeping to the left of farm buildings, look out for a yellow waymark on a tree in front which indicates a turn to the left. Head down a field to climb a stile, descend a flight of steps and continue along the left-hand edge of a field, by a hedge and wire fence on the left, passing Caplor Farm on the left. Follow the field edge as it curves first right and then left down to a stile in the bottom left-hand corner, climb it, bear left along the edge of the next field, climb another stile and turn right along a tarmac drive to a road (G).

Turn left and after about 50 yards (46 m) turn right, at a Wye Valley Walk signpost,

along a broad track. Where the track bends to the right turn right onto a narrow path along the left-hand edge of a field, following the field edge round to the right and turning left over a stile. Turn right and after a few yards bear left along the right-hand edge of a field, with a hedge on the right, heading gently downhill along a narrow and sometimes overgrown path. At the bottom end follow the field edge round to the left, at a yellow waymark turn right through a metal gate and continue uphill along the left-hand edge of a field, by a hedge and wire fence on the left. Climb a stile and head gently uphill along the left-hand edge of the next field, continuing over a series of stiles and keeping along the left-hand edge of fields to enter Paget's Wood, a Herefordshire Nature Trust reserve.

Follow a path through this delightful area of woodland, climbing a stile beside a metal gate and keeping ahead to emerge from the wood. Continue along the edge of a field, bearing slightly right and heading uphill, by a wire fence and the edge of the woodland on the right, to climb a stile onto a lane.

Cross over and keep ahead, by a Wye Valley Walk signpost, passing to the right of Common Hill Farm, and at a fork a few yards ahead bear left along a hedge-enclosed track and turn right over a stile at a yellow waymark. Turn left along a very pleasant, narrow path that winds through more attractive woodland and from a thoughtfully provided bench later on there is a magnificent view over the Wye Valley with Fownhope church in the foreground. From the viewpoint the path continues downhill, over a stile and ahead to a junction of tracks. Here take the second turning on the left, head downhill to join a narrow lane (H) and continue along it for ¾ mile (1·25 km) to descend into Fownhope.

Brockhampton's highly distinctive early twentieth-century church

22 Tintern Abbey and the Devil's Pulpit

Start:	Tintern
Distance:	7 miles (11·25 km)
Approximate time:	3½ hours
Parking:	Parking spaces beside road at Tintern
Refreshments:	Pubs and cafés at Tintern, pub at Brockweir, café at Tintern Station
Ordnance Survey maps:	Landranger 162 (Gloucester & Forest of Dean) and Outdoor Leisure 14 (Wye Valley & Forest of Dean)

General description

*Once again do I behold these steep and
   lofty cliffs,
That on a wild secluded scene impress
Thoughts of more deep seclusion; and
   connect
The landscape with the quiet of the sky.
Oh sylvan Wye! thou wanderer thro' the
   woods,
How often has my spirit turned to thee.*

*Apart from the considerably reduced
seclusion, the landscape around Tintern
Abbey can have changed little since it
inspired Wordsworth to compose these lines
in 1798. Every ingredient that goes to create a
varied, satisfying and memorable walk is
present here: a peaceful riverside path below
steep wooded cliffs, a climb through most
attractive woodland to a magnificent vantage
point, a descent across more open country
and a final relaxing stroll across meadows
bordering the Wye. As an added bonus there
is of course Tintern Abbey itself, one of the
most beautiful and superbly situated
monastic remains in the country.*

Begin by walking southwards along the main
road and soon Tintern Abbey comes into
sight. Its setting on the Welsh side of the
river, with the steep and thickly wooded cliffs
that rise from the opposite English bank
making a dramatic backcloth, could hardly be
bettered. Tintern was a Cistercian
monastery, founded by Walter de Clare, Lord
of Chepstow in 1131, and had an apparently
uneventful history until its dissolution by
Henry VIII in 1536. The remains are most
impressive, especially the majestic church,
rebuilt in the late thirteenth century, which is
almost intact save for roofs and windows. Its
walls still rise to their full height, much of the

delicate window tracery survives, especially
on the large and ornate west window, and
the graceful Gothic arches of both the nave
and choir look particularly attractive when
the sun casts alternating patterns of light and
shade across the now grassy floors.

Continue along the road if you wish to visit
the abbey. Otherwise take the first turning on
the left (**A**), passing Abbey Mill on the right,
and cross the footbridge over the River Wye.
Continue along the wooded track ahead,
which curves to the right to run roughly
parallel to the river, and keep along this track,
once part of the picturesque Wye Valley
Railway, for nearly 2 miles (3·25 km), at the
base of wooded cliffs on the left and with the
river on the right. Gaps in the trees in the
initial stages provide a few glimpses of the
river and abbey ruins.

Take the left-hand track at a fork, following
the direction of yellow arrows,. climbing
gently to the next yellow waymark. Here turn
sharp left (**B**) along an uphill track, following
a permissive route and looking out for yellow
waymarks all the time, to reach a T-junction
of tracks. Cross over and take the narrow
path ahead that leads steeply uphill through
dense but most attractive woodland to
another T-junction. Turn left and head
slightly downhill to a waymark and here turn
right along a narrow, winding, uphill, stepped
path. At the next waymark you join Offa's
Dyke Path (**C**); keep ahead and follow it as it
twists and turns through the trees high above
the valley to arrive at the glorious vantage
point of the Devil's Pulpit. Here a strategically
placed seat enables you to appreciate in
comfort the view over the Wye Valley to the
wooded slopes beyond, with the abbey ruins
picturesquely sited immediately below.
According to legend, the Devil tried to entice
the monks from their duties at this spot,
hence its name.

Continue above the valley, with the
glorious view in sight most of the time, and
through more lovely woodland, following
Offa's Dyke Path waymarks all the while and
soon starting to descend. At a signpost
ignore the left-hand turn to Tintern and keep
ahead along Offa's Dyke Path, following the
signs to Brockweir and St Briavels, later
going down steps to a gate. Go through and
keep straight ahead at a junction of paths,
now heading gently downhill along the right-
hand edge of woodland and bearing right to a
stile. Climb it, continue along the top edge of
the valley and at an Offa's Dyke Path
waymark bear left away from the wire fence
on the right along a rocky path which heads
downhill.

Continue in a straight line across a field, in
the direction indicated by yellow-topped
posts, and at the bottom corner turn left by a
now redundant stile to pick up a broad track.

Head down to a signpost where Offa's Dyke Path divides and keep ahead (**D**) in the direction of the sign 'Offa's Dyke Path via River Wye'. Go through a gate, on through another one and continue, passing farm buildings on the right, to go through yet another gate and down to another signpost. Ignoring the left-hand turn to Tintern on the signpost, turn right between farm buildings and continue along a tarmac drive to the road at Brockweir (**E**).

Turn left along the road, cross the river and turn left over a stile, at a public footpath sign to Tintern, to descend steps. At the bottom there is a choice of routes. One route is to turn left, climb a stile and then turn right to follow a pleasant path across riverside meadows. The alternative is to keep along the track straight ahead, which passes through the disused Tintern Station, to rejoin the riverside path by the supports of a former railway bridge. The old Victorian station at Tintern has been attractively restored as a visitor and information centre and picnic site, and provides refreshments.

Where the two alternative routes reunite, climb a stile and keep along the riverbank, curving right to cross a footbridge over a ditch and continuing up to another stile. Climb over, walk through the churchyard of Tintern's small parish church and follow yellow arrows between houses to the main road. Keep ahead to return to the parking area.

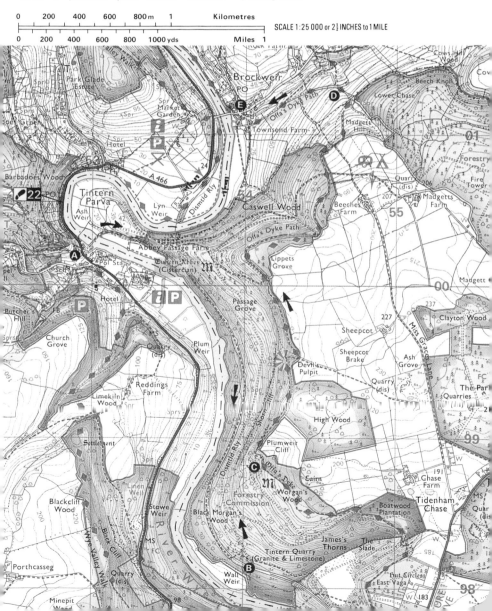

| 0 | 200 | 400 | 600 | 800 m | 1 | Kilometres |

SCALE 1:25 000 or 2½ INCHES to 1 MILE

| 0 | 200 | 400 | 600 | 800 | 1000 yds | Miles 1 |

23 Speech House, Cannop Ponds and Edge End

Start:	Forestry Commission car park and picnic area at Speech House Woodland
Distance:	8½ miles (13·5 km)
Approximate time:	4½ hours
Parking:	Speech House Woodland car park
Refreshments:	Speech House Hotel
Ordnance Survey maps:	Landranger 162 (Gloucester & Forest of Dean) and Outdoor Leisure 14 (Wye Valley & Forest of Dean)

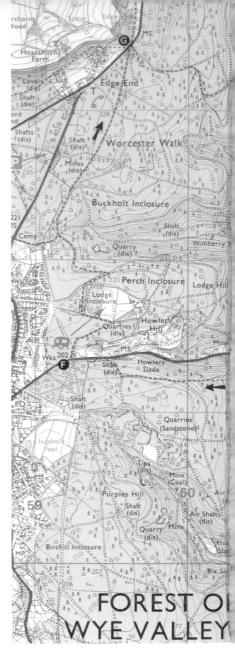

General description *Some of the finest deciduous woodlands in the Forest of Dean are to be found around the Speech House, in the heart of the forest, and much of this splendid walk passes through a landscape that has probably changed little since the days of the medieval royal forest. There are a few short stretches of modern conifer forest, and two welcome modern additions which only enhance the traditional woodland: the attractive Cannop Ponds and a striking piece of forest sculpture. This is quite an energetic walk with several climbs but with the compensation of some superb views from the higher points.*

From the car park, itself a charming spot of widely spaced oaks and grassy glades, take the path through the trees opposite the toilet block, keeping parallel to the road on the left. After climbing a stile the Speech House can be seen on the left. A few yards further on turn left (**A**), climb another stile and head up to the road opposite the Speech House. This handsome building, now a hotel, was built in 1676 by Charles II to serve as the new headquarters for the royal forest, a hunting-lodge and a meeting place for the Verderers' Court, known alternatively as the 'Court of Speech', hence its name. The former Court Room, now the dining room of the hotel, is still periodically used for meetings of the Verderers, maintaining a longstanding historic tradition.

Take the road ahead by the right-hand side of the Speech House, signposted to Park End, Yorkley and Blakeney, passing a number of commemorative trees on the right, and at a Forestry Commission notice saying 'Speech House Arboretum Car Park and

Picnic Place' bear left along a broad track. Go through a gate and continue along the straight track ahead, called the Spruce Ride. When you see a small lake through the trees on the right, turn right and take a path along the left-hand side of Speech House Lake, which was formed by the damming of Blackpool Brook in 1974 to create a wildlife reserve. Bear right around the end of the lake and turn left along a narrow path, initially

```
0    200  400  600  800 m   1        Kilometres
0    200  400  600  800  1000 yds    Miles 1
```

between gorse bushes, that keeps by the right-hand side of the brook to reach a junction of tracks (**B**).

Turn right along a track that heads gently uphill to a stile, climb it, cross a road and continue along the track directly opposite. A few yards before a gate turn right over a stile in a wire fence, then turn left to rejoin the track and follow it downhill to a junction of five tracks. This is a very attractive part of the route, passing through an area of widely spaced broad-leaved trees and small glades of grass and fern on the right, with views beyond of the densely wooded slopes on the other side of the Cannop valley. At the junction there were originally three tall oaks side by side called the Three Brothers; now there are only two, the third one just a stump.

Turn right here (**C**) along a track indicated by a green-waymarked post, heading gently

The Speech House — former forest headquarters surrounded by fine woodland

downhill to a stile. Climb it and continue through more fine traditional woodland, the trees on the left rising above a carpet of bluebells and fern. Bear right and then turn left at a post with both green and yellow waymarks to cross the track of a disused railway and continue to the southern end of Cannop Ponds. To the left is a stone works, the last of its kind surviving in the Forest of Dean. Do not cross the footbridge over the outlet stream but turn right (**D**) to follow a most attractive path along the right-hand edge of the lower pond which keeps parallel to the disused railway track above a low embankment on the right — the latter can be used as a flatter and slightly easier alternative.

From this point the rest of the route follows yellow waymarks, mostly arrows on tree trunks. Shortly after the lower pond peters out you reach a fork; take the left-hand path to enter a small clearing, keep ahead into another larger clearing — a picnic site — and turn left (**E**) over a footbridge at the bottom end of the upper pond, continuing to a road. The two ponds were formed in the early nineteenth century by damming Cannop Brook to provide water power for the nearby iron works at Parkend. Although the iron works were abandoned and demolished in 1908, the ponds remain as an attractive scenic feature, adding variety to an area of thick, almost unbroken woodland.

Cross the road, walk through a small parking area opposite and briefly take the track ahead which almost immediately turns to the right. At this point keep straight ahead between thick conifers, heading uphill, cross a green track and continue up to another one. Cross that and now climb more steeply between tall Douglas firs, crossing another track and keeping ahead — this part of the walk is decidedly gloomy — to emerge briefly into an area of mixed woodland. Here the path flattens out before plunging again into thick conifers. On reaching a broad, grassy track turn right along it to a forest barrier and continue to the track junction beyond; here

keep ahead along a path that passes by a redundant stile. Take the right-hand path at a fork and continue to another junction of paths, here turning right down to the road (**F**) opposite a Forestry Commission sign 'Worcester Lodge Camp Site'.

Cross over, take the tarmac drive ahead, and just after the drive curves to the right look out for yellow waymarks which indicate a left turn along a narrow path across an area of mixed woodland. Passing to the left of the camp site, continue along what is now a much wider path and at the corner of the camp site boundary the path bears right to join a grassy track. Follow the track as far as the next track and here turn sharp left. This bends first to the right, then curves left and bends right again to continue in a straight line. Just before the next gentle curve to the right look out for several yellow waymarks on tree-trunks and follow them to bear left off this track along a path that leads to a stile. Climb it and continue to the gate ahead, climbing another stile a few yards to the left of it. Now walk along a track to a junction and keep ahead to reach a forestry barrier beside the road at Edge End (**G**). On the other side of the road there is a superb view looking across the Wye Valley to the Black Mountains on the horizon.

Turn right, at a footpath sign to Speech House, along another broad track, with more fine open views to the right, following it as it bends to the right and heads downhill. Just before reaching the bottom of the hill, where the track starts to curve to the left and opposite a stile on the right, turn left along a path which shortly crosses a track and continues straight ahead, then bears right and heads downhill. Keep ahead at a crossroads of paths, soon bearing right and continuing down to a track. (If you miss this last turning it does not matter — you still reach the track, where you just turn right to regain the yellow waymarked route in a few yards.) Cross over the track and head gently downhill, crossing another track and continuing to a road (**H**).

Cross the road, keep ahead over the stepping-stones over Cannop Brook — a delightful spot — and continue, climbing steeply to cross the disused railway track again. Climb a stile and take the uphill path ahead, bearing left by the left-hand side of a quarry to continue along an uphill track. Keep ahead at a crossroads, passing to the left of the Giant Chair, a dramatic piece of forest sculpture from where there is a fine and extensive view over the thickly wooded Cannop valley. Continue to a stile but do not climb it; instead turn right and head uphill towards the Speech House. Turn left in front of a stile, climb another one and retrace your steps to the car park.

24 Bredwardine, Arthur's Stone and Dorstone

Start: Bredwardine

Distance: 7½ miles (12 km). Shorter version 5 miles (8 km)

Approximate time: 4 hours (3 hours for shorter version)

Parking: Verges along lane leading to church at Bredwardine

Refreshments: Pub at Bredwardine, pub at Dorstone

Ordnance Survey maps: Landranger 161 (Abergavenny & the Black Mountains) and Pathfinder 1016, SO 24/34 (Hay-on-Wye)

General description *Bredwardine and Dorstone hills form part of a broad ridge that rises to almost 1,000 feet (305 m), separating the Wye and Golden valleys. Bredwardine is situated at the foot of the ridge's eastern flanks in the Wye Valley, Dorstone lies below its western slopes in the Golden Valley, and Arthur's Stone, a prehistoric burial chamber, occupies the top of the ridge. These are the three focal points of a walk that involves two quite lengthy and reasonably steep climbs. The route mostly uses country lanes as many of the footpaths in the area are narrow and overgrown, blocked by crops or lacking in gates and stiles, and waymarking is almost non-existent. As these lanes are quiet, little used by vehicles, and provide magnificent views over both valleys, especially from the top of the ridge and on the two descents, this makes for a thoroughly worthwhile walk amidst splendid scenery. The shorter version of the walk omits Dorstone.*

Refer to map overleaf.

Francis Kilvert was the rector of Bredwardine for the last two years of his life and is buried in the churchyard of the partially Norman church that has a pleasing but rather asymmetrical appearance, chiefly due to the late eighteenth-century north-western tower. The village occupies an attractive position above the River Wye which is crossed by a fine eighteenth-century bridge. In the meadows to the south of the church are some earthworks and the remains of the fishponds of the medieval castle.

Start at the crossroads in the centre of the village by the seventeenth-century Red Lion Inn. With your back to the inn walk down the lane signposted to Staunton-on-Wye, bearing right along a tarmac track at a Wye Valley Walk waymark and sign to Bredwardine church. In front of the church turn right along a grassy track, go through a metal gate and keep ahead across a field, veering slightly right to the far right-hand corner. Here continue along a winding, undulating path – some of the earthworks of the now vanished Bredwardine Castle are on the left – keeping along the right-hand edge of woodland. Go through a gate, descend, passing to the right of a pond, and continue, going through a gap in a wire fence, bearing right and heading gently uphill to pass through a metal gate. Continue along the right-hand edge of a field, by a hedge on the right, bearing gradually right to go through another metal gate onto a road.

Turn right, take the first turning on the left (**A**), signposted 'Dorstone via Dorstone Hill', and follow the narrow, twisting, uphill lane, which is steep in parts, for about ¾ mile (1·25 km). Just below the top turn right along an even narrower lane (**B**), signposted to Arthur's Stone, continuing uphill onto the ridge. From this lane, that runs along the top of the broad ridge between the Wye and Golden valleys, there are magnificent views on both sides: to the right over the Wye Valley and to the left over the Golden Valley to the Black Mountains on the horizon. After ¼ mile (0·5 km) you reach Arthur's Stone (**C**), which has nothing to do with King Arthur but is an impressive, late Neolithic chambered tomb, dating from around 2000 to 3000 BC. It was originally covered with a mound of earth and has a massive capstone about 20 feet (6 m) long.

At this point, those wishing to do only the shorter version of the walk can continue along the lane, following the route after (C) below.

Turn left through a metal gate at a footpath sign and head downhill in a straight line, initially across the middle of two fields, with a glorious view over the Golden Valley ahead all the while. Continue along the right-hand edge of the next two fields, then pass through a metal gate on the right and keep along the left-hand edge of several more fields to reach a road. Turn right, crossing the tiny and almost invisible River Dore, turn left (**D**) at a signpost to Dorstone and then take the first turning on the right, passing a row of attractive cottages with colourful gardens, to arrive at the charming, peaceful village green at Dorstone. Nearby is the mound of the former motte and bailey castle.

At the green turn right along a lane signposted 'Dorstone Church – No Through

0   200   400   600   800 m   1   Kilometres

0   200   400   600   800   1000 yds   Miles   1

SCALE 1:25 000 or 2½ INCHES to 1 MILE

Road' and take a tarmac lane to the left of the churchyard up to the road. Dorstone's church was rebuilt in the late nineteenth century but stands on an ancient site. Turn right along the road, later retracing your steps uphill to Arthur's Stone (C).

Here turn left (those on the shorter walk carry straight on) to continue along the straight ridge-top lane, later following it around a number of sharp right-hand bends and descending gently back into the Wye Valley. Where the lane bends sharply to the left (E) you can either continue along the lane for an easy return to Bredwardine or, for a more scenic though possibly more muddy route, turn right along a tarmac track signposted 'Fine Street'. Almost immediately turn left down a rough track and where it bears left towards a house negotiate a rather broken-down stile in front and head diagonally downhill across a steeply sloping field, from where there is a splendid view over the Wye Valley with Bredwardine church a prominent landmark.

Make for a belt of trees in the bottom corner, cross a stream and go through a metal gate a few yards ahead. Continue diagonally across the next field, go through another gate onto a track and follow this hedge-lined track back to Bredwardine, coming out onto the road at the side of the Red Lion Inn.

25 St Briavels and Hewelsfield

Start:	St Briavels
Distance:	8 miles (12·75 km)
Approximate time:	4 hours
Parking:	Near entrance to St Briavels Castle
Refreshments:	Pubs at St Briavels
Ordnance Survey maps:	Landranger 162 (Gloucester & Forest of Dean) and Outdoor Leisure 14 (Wye Valley & Forest of Dean)

General description *From St Briavels, high up on the edge of the Forest of Dean from where there are glorious views over the Wye Valley, the route first descends into the valley and then continues along a fairly energetic stretch of Offa's Dyke Path, passing some well-preserved sections of the dyke itself, before climbing up to the village of Hewelsfield. From here a delightful, secluded, enclosed track, overgrown in places but easily walkable, leads back to St Briavels. As well as extensive views there is considerable historic interest on the walk: St Briavels Castle, the fine medieval churches at both St Briavels and Hewelsfield and of course Offa's Dyke. There are two climbs; the first is quite steep and the second more gradual.*

Refer to map overleaf.

The village centre at St Briavels makes a delightful scene, dominated by the castle around whose walls old cottages, village shops and the pub are grouped in a circle, and opposite the impressive castle gatehouse is the imposing twelfth- to thirteenth-century cruciform church. Both the castle and church are indications that this small village was once a place of much greater importance. In the Middle Ages St Briavels was the administrative centre of the Royal Forest of Dean and its thirteenth-century castle, which has a commanding position above the Wye Valley, was a combination of border stronghold, royal hunting lodge, prison and court. Nowadays it serves a much more peaceful function as part of it is a youth hostel.

Start by the church and castle gatehouse, from where there is a magnificent view over the Wye Valley, and bear right along the downhill lane signposted to Lower Meend. Bear right again at a fork, at a junction of lanes turn sharply to the right and after a few yards turn equally sharply to the left, at a public footpath sign, along a narrow, downhill hedge-lined path. Follow the direction of a red waymark down some steps by a house on the left and continue along the path to a lane (**A**).

Turn right down this steep, narrow lane between the cottages of Lower Meend, and just in front of the gates of a sewage works bear left through trees to go through a yellow-waymarked gate. Bear right along the right-hand edge of a field, turn right through a metal gate at the bottom end of the field and then turn left along a track that leads to Lindors Farm. Pass to the right of the farm buildings and continue along the track, going through a succession of gates and heading steadily downhill all the while. There are fine views ahead of the thickly wooded slopes that rise from the Welsh side of the Wye, and to the right and left of the wooded hills of the Forest of Dean.

Just before reaching the road by Bigsweir Bridge (**B**) turn sharp left along a broad track to join Offa's Dyke Path — the next section of the walk is well-waymarked with Offa's Dyke Path signs and the acorn symbol. After passing over a cattle-grid bear left and head diagonally uphill across a large sloping field, making for the top corner, here crossing a recognisable and well-preserved section of Offa's Dyke. Climb a stile, continue more gently uphill across the next field towards the woodland ahead, climb another stile and follow a path through this dense but most attractive woodland, almost immediately bearing left where the path forks. Now comes the toughest part of the walk. Head steeply uphill, looking out for yellow waymarks on rocks and tree-trunks, climb some wooden steps by a handrail, continue to the top of the cliff and here turn sharp right. Bear left along an enclosed path, between walls both sides, heading now more gently uphill towards a large house on the left.

Here turn right (**C**) along a tarmac lane, keeping slightly left at a fork, and at an Offa's Dyke Path signpost to Brockweir and Sedbury Cliff turn right along a track which bears left in front of a house. At a fork take the left-hand track which continues to a lane (**D**), turn right down the lane and just after passing a farm on the left turn left over a stile in a hedge. Keep ahead to a marker-post, continue past it to climb two stiles in quick succession and then follow a grassy path to another stile. Climb that, keep ahead a few yards and then bear slightly left to join a hedge-lined track, shortly turning right onto a path. This path curves to the left and heads gently downhill — it runs between walls and hedges and is pleasantly tree-lined — to reach some houses. Here bear right and

continue down a tarmac drive to a lane (**E**). Turn left down the lane, following it as it curves to the left, and at a signpost to Brockweir and Sedbury Cliff turn right along another tree-lined path. This descends gently, crosses a lane and continues downhill to another lane; here turn left for a few yards and then turn right along a track. Where the track bears left continue along a path, cross a

stream and keep ahead to join first another track and then a road a few yards ahead (**F**).

Cross the road — at this point leaving Offa's Dyke Path — and take the broad, wooded track in front that heads downhill to join and keep by a brook on the right. Where the track curves left to a house continue straight ahead along an enclosed, tree-lined path that climbs up to reach a lane (**G**). Turn

The lovely little forest church at Hewelsfield

right along this narrow, wooded lane, heading gently uphill, keep ahead on joining a wider lane and continue up to the village of Hewelsfield.

Keep straight ahead at a crossroads along a lane that curves gently to the right to reach the delightful and unusual church. This impressive cruciform building, of Saxon origin, possesses a fine Norman nave and a thirteenth-century chancel. The central tower is squat and massive looking but the most striking feature of the exterior is the roof of the nave that slopes so steeply that it almost reaches the ground.

Bear left, passing to the left of the church, and where the lane curves gently to the right bear left (**H**) again down a narrow lane to where that bends to the right. Here turn left, go through a metal gate by a barn on the right and on along a track to climb a half-hidden stile by a metal gate.

Continue along a sunken, partially overgrown, enclosed path — an almost forgotten byway that has a grand feeling of remoteness. Climb a stone stile, keep ahead along the left-hand edge of a field, by a line of trees and wire fence on the left — there are extensive views to the right here over the forest — and bear slightly right at the end of the field to pass through a gap in a fence by a yellow waymark. Walk along what now becomes an enclosed tree-lined path again, climb a stone stile beside a metal gate, keep ahead, passing to the left of a farm, and cross a farm drive. Continue along a broad track, beside a belt of woodland on the left, to a stile. Climb that and another one a few yards ahead and keep more or less in a straight line along the right-hand edge of a series of fields, climbing a succession of stiles. From this elevated position there are pleasant views all around.

When the houses of St Briavels come into view look out for and turn right over a stile in a hedge, beside a house, descend a few steps and turn left along a lane, between modern housing, to a road junction (**J**). Cross over and keep ahead, shortly bearing right by the Crown Inn to return to the village centre and castle entrance.

26 Sugar Loaf

Start:	National Trust car park at Sugar Loaf, about 2½ miles (4 km) north-west of Abergavenny and signposted from the A40
Distance:	5½ miles (8·75 km)
Approximate time:	3 hours
Parking:	Sugar Loaf car park
Refreshments:	None
Ordnance Survey maps:	Landranger 161 (Abergavenny & the Black Mountains) and Outdoor Leisure 13 (Brecon Beacons — Eastern area)

General description *Sugar Loaf is the prominent, conical-shaped hill that rises 1,955 feet (596 m) above the Usk valley to the north-west of Abergavenny. Its smooth, grass- and bracken-covered slopes are criss-crossed by paths and tracks, making both the ascent and descent enjoyable and relatively easy, though this myriad of paths can also be somewhat confusing, especially in misty conditions. This is therefore a walk best set aside for a fine, clear day, when the superb views from the summit can be enjoyed to the full. Almost the whole of this walk is on land owned by the National Trust.*

At 1,132 feet (345 m) the National Trust car park takes a lot of the hard work out of this climb as well as providing an immediate grand viewpoint over the Usk valley to Blorenge (the hill on the opposite side), the Black Mountains and Brecon Beacons. A toposcope points out all the places that can be seen from here.

With your back to the view over the valley turn half-left, at a public footpath sign, along a broad path and follow it gently uphill between bracken and gorse. On meeting a wall the path forks; take the left-hand path, continuing uphill with the distinctive summit of Sugar Loaf to the right. At the next fork, about 100 yards (91 m) ahead, take the right-hand path, go straight on at a crossroads of paths and after a while the path bends right to another crossroads. Here turn left along a steadily ascending path which curves to the right, keeping ahead at a crossroads, later climbing more steeply and finally scrambling between boulders to reach the triangulation pillar at the summit (**A**).

From this isolated outlier a magnificent all-round view unfolds. To the west lie the Brecon Beacons, to the north across the Black Mountains the rolling farmlands of Herefordshire can be seen, to the south-east Abergavenny lies immediately below and beyond that the view stretches to the coast and across the Bristol Channel to the hills of Avon and Somerset on the horizon. Looking to the south across the Usk valley a few signs of industrial South Wales can be made out.

At the summit turn right along the ridge

The distinctive but easily climbed bulk of the Sugar Loaf

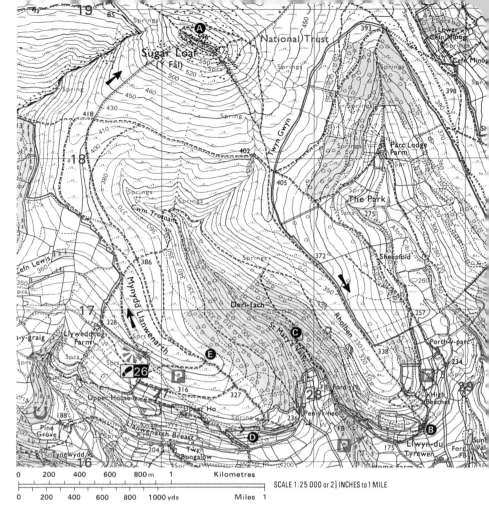

and near the end bear right to drop steeply from the summit cone. Keep in the same direction — south-easterly — along a curving downhill path, between bilberries, heather and bracken, over a small stream and down to a crossroads of paths. Continue in a straight line downhill, by a wire fence on the left, finally descending steeply between bracken to a lane (**B**). On this part of the walk there are impressive views of Ysgyryd Fawr to the left and Blorenge in front — two of the three hills (Sugar Loaf being the third) that cradle Abergavenny.

Continue along this rough, narrow lane, climbing a stile beside a gate and heading gently downhill to a T-junction; here turn right along an uphill and equally narrow lane. Pass by a small parking area on the left and at the fork just ahead take the left-hand track, between wire fences both sides, passing a house on the right and continuing into woodland.

Now follows a most beautiful section of the walk through the idyllic woodlands that clothe the steep sides of St Mary's Vale on the southern slopes of Sugar Loaf. Cross a footbridge over a stream and, ignoring a stile on the left, keep ahead through the woods — the stream is now on the right — to where a track comes in from the left. Turn sharp left (**C**), almost doubling back, along this track which heads gently uphill, emerging from the woods and continuing for ¼ mile (0·5 km) to a lane. Bear right uphill along this lane, signposted Sugar Loaf, for ¼ mile (0·5 km), looking out for where a steep track descends to it from the right just by a passing place.

Turn sharp right (**D**) onto the track and follow it uphill between bracken, soon curving to the left. At a junction bear left to continue in a north-westerly direction over the lower slopes of Sugar Loaf, with more fine views over the Usk valley to the left, and very shortly the summit can be seen again on the right. At the second crossroads (**E**), where the track ahead continues as a dual track, bear left and head gently downhill to rejoin the lane, turning right for the short distance back to the car park.

27 Llanthony Priory and Hatterrall Hill

Start:	Llanthony Priory
Distance:	8 miles (12·75 km)
Approximate time:	4 ½ hours
Parking:	Car park at Llanthony Priory
Refreshments:	Abbey Hotel at Llanthony Priory
Ordnance Survey maps:	Landranger 161 (Abergavenny & the Black Mountains) and Outdoor Leisure 13 (Brecon Beacons — Eastern area)

General description *The Vale of Ewyas, a long, narrow, quiet valley on the eastern edge of the Black Mountains, provides a secluded and romantic setting for the grand ruins of Llanthony Priory. From the ruins, the route heads southwards along the western edge of the valley before crossing the River Honddu to the hamlet of Cwmyoy. Then a lengthy but not particularly steep or strenuous climb over Hatterrall Hill to join Offa's Dyke Path is followed by a superb ridge walk along the Welsh — English border. From the ridge there are the most magnificent views westwards over the Black Mountains and eastwards across the Herefordshire plain. The spectacular descent back into the valley has the priory in sight for most of the time to conclude a truly memorable walk. Because route-finding on the latter part of the climb over Hatterrall Hill could be difficult in misty weather, it is recommended that the walk should be done only in clear conditions, unless walkers are experienced in using a compass.*

The restrained, austere-looking ruins of Llanthony Priory, in the peaceful, lonely Vale of Ewyas and enclosed by the bare slopes of the Black Mountains, match their setting perfectly. The Augustinian priory was founded in the early twelfth century, and much of the late twelfth- and early thirteenth-century church survives — notably the west front, north arcade of the nave, central tower and parts of the east end. Little remains of the domestic buildings, although the small parish church nearby incorporates the monks' infirmary. Uniquely the south-west tower of the priory church is now the Abbey Hotel, surely one of the most unusually sited hotels in the country.

From the car park walk down the lane to the road, turn left and almost immediately

bear right along a track, at a public footpath sign to Bal Bach. Climb a stile, bear left to cross a footbridge over the River Honddu, climb the left-hand one of two stiles in front and walk along the right-hand edge of a field, by a line of trees and wire fence on the right. Where the fence veers to the right, veer right through a gap in the trees, cross a brook and head gently uphill in a straight line across a field to climb a stile. Continue uphill across the next field, crossing a track, climb a stile and keep ahead to climb another stile in the top corner of the next field.

Turn left onto a track that keeps along the side of the valley, go through a gate and ahead is a fork. Take the right-hand track through the conifer plantations of Llanthony Wood — after passing a house on the right the track narrows to a path — later rejoining a track and following it to a gate. Go through to leave the wood, continue along the track to where it starts to ascend and curve to the right, here keeping ahead along a grassy downhill track, by a wire fence on the left. To the left is a fine view of Hatterrall Hill which drops down abruptly into the valley.

Go through a metal gate and continue, keeping to the right of farm buildings, to pass through another metal gate and on along a very pleasant track by the left-hand edge of more woodland. After going through another metal gate keep ahead across rough ground, making for and bearing left along a broad track that comes in from the right. Pass to the right of farm buildings and just before reaching a gate in front bear left off the track along a thankfully short section of narrow, indistinct and overgrown path to a yellow-waymarked stile. Climb it and continue along the top right-hand edge of a sloping field — there are plenty of signs here to keep you on the correct route — following a pleasantly shady tree-lined path by the edge of woodland on the right. Climb two stiles, entering the wood after the second one, and follow a path through it, climbing another stile at the far end. Continue along a narrow path between bracken, passing a house on the left, climb a stile and follow the track ahead, heading gently downhill and curving left to climb another stile onto a road (**A**).

Turn left, take the first turning on the right, at a public footpath sign to Cwmyoy, recross the River Honddu and take the track ahead (**B**). About 50 yards (46 m) after passing a house on the left turn left up some steps, at a footpath sign, to a stile. Climb it, cross a track and keep ahead to climb another stile. Continue along the right-hand edge of a field above the wooded riverbank on the right, climb a stile and keep ahead, by a hedge on the right, to go through a metal gate. Continue along the left-hand edge of a field, with a hedge on the left, go through a metal

SCALE 1:25 000 or 2½ INCHES to 1 MILE

73

gate and keep along the field edge to another gate. Go through that and continue along the left-hand edge of the next field but before reaching the end of it veer right and head across to a metal gate. Pass through that, keep ahead by the river, go through another metal gate and continue to a lane a few yards ahead. Turn left along this narrow uphill lane, which curves to the right and continues into the hamlet of Cwmyoy.

Bear left along an uphill lane signposted 'No Through Road' and turn left (**C**) into the churchyard. Cymyoy church is a lovely old building in a tranquil and isolated setting; it is plain, simple and pleasantly irregular, the latter the result of slight subsidence in the underlying rock. It is an ancient foundation and up to the dissolution of the monasteries was served by the monks from Llanthony.

Turn right by the east end of the church, head up to a metal gate, go through and bear left along a track for a few yards to a footpath sign. Here turn right along a steep, uphill, enclosed path, go through a metal gate and turn right, keeping by a wire fence and broken-down wall on the right, passing below a rock face and continuing by a more substantial wall on the right to a T-junction of paths. Turn left and head uphill, by a wall on the right; after passing a cottage on the left the path levels out and continues by a wire fence on the right.

Follow this pleasant and partially wooded path over two stiles to a metal gate. Go through it, continue towards the ridge in front and where the wire fence on the right ends keep ahead along a clear path through an area of trees and bracken to go through another metal gate. Cross a stream and continue uphill for a few yards to a track. Turn left along this grassy, uphill track which shortly bends to the right — there is a grand view down the valley from here — passing through a metal gate, curving to the left and continuing to wind upwards between the bracken, bilberries and heather of Hatterrall Hill towards the ridge. After a while the track narrows to a path which later runs parallel to and just below the top of the ridge on the right. There are glorious views to the left through a gap in the hills, looking towards the coast of South Wales and beyond the Bristol Channel to the hills of Avon and Somerset on the horizon. At this stage the route becomes a little confusing, as there are lots of sheep tracks and the exact path may be difficult to distinguish, but continue in a northerly direction, making for the top of the ridge, to reach a broad track near two cairns. It does not matter if you reach the track at some other point — it is so wide and clearly defined that you cannot miss it.

Turn left along the track (**D**), here joining Offa's Dyke Path, for a magnificent 1¾-mile (3 km) ridge walk that provides the most outstanding and contrasting views. To the right, across rolling heathery moorland, is the Herefordshire plain and beyond that the Cotswolds and Malverns — a lovely patchwork of fields of green and gold and small woodlands, English landscape at its finest. To the left is a contrasting view over the Honddu valley, the head of it cradled by the bare slopes of the Black Mountains, to the outline of the Brecon Beacons. Offa's Dyke Path here forms the boundary between Wales and England and there could hardly be a more distinctive frontier — the transition between lowland England and upland Wales, the frontier between Saxon and Celt. As an added bonus the priory ruins can soon be seen below on the left.

When you see a wall corner over to the left bear left (**E**), at a small cairn, along a grassy path, heading for that corner and then continuing by a wall on the left. The path soon starts to descend through bracken and above woodland on the left — there are glorious views of the priory almost all the time from now on. Later the path keeps by a wire fence on the left; look out for a yellow-waymarked stile on the left, climb it and head downhill along the left-hand edge of a field, by a wire fence on the left, to climb a stile into Wiral Wood. Bear right to follow a broad track through the wood, later bearing left and heading down to another stile. Climb it and turn right along a field edge, by a wire fence and the edge of the wood on the right, following the field edge downhill and round to the left to climb a stile in the bottom corner. Keeping by the priory wall on the left, climb another stile and turn left to pass the west front of the church, turning left again over a stile to return to the car park.

Descent to Llanthony Priory in the secluded Vale of Ewyas

28 Symonds Yat and Highmeadow Woods

Start:	Forestry Commission car park at Symonds Yat Rock
Distance:	9 miles (14·5 km). Shorter version 8 miles (12·75 km)
Approximate time:	4½ hours (4 hours for shorter version)
Parking:	Symonds Yat Rock car park
Refreshments:	Café at car park, pub at Staunton
Ordnance Survey maps:	Landranger 162 (Gloucester & Forest of Dean) and Outdoor Leisure 14 (Wye Valley & Forest of Dean)

General description *Much of this spendid and quite energetic walk is through delightful woodland, with occasional forays into more open country that provide superb views over the forest, Wye Valley and beyond. Highmeadow Woods are an outlying part of the Forest of Dean, occupying an area of high ground roughly between Monmouth, Symonds Yat and Coleford. They were originally part of the medieval forest, later passed into private ownership and returned to Crown possession in 1817. The walk links together a series of prominent outcrops of rock which act as the main focal points, and in some cases viewpoints. The most magnificent view is the classic one over the winding River Wye from Symonds Yat, which you can enjoy either at the start or finish. There are some fairly stiff climbs and some tortuous sections along narrow forest paths but fortunately the route is well-waymarked with yellow arrows; you will still need to keep a sharp lookout, however, as some of the arrows painted on trees are not always obvious. The shorter version of the walk omits the viewpoint of the Buck Stone.*

Refer to map overleaf.

Symonds Yat Rock rises 500 feet (152 m) above the Wye and from it there is a spectacular view over the winding river, one of the finest views in the country, familiar as a favourite choice for birthday cards, calendars and chocolate-box covers. The Wye can be seen in almost every direction, which seems confusing but is the result of

the many great loops that the river makes in the vicinity of the rock.

Start by the Log Cabin Refreshment Hut in the car park and follow the yellow-waymarked path that bears left past it, heading steeply downhill through the trees. This narrow, twisting, rocky path, stepped in places, turns left at a signpost marked 'Symonds Yat East and Riverside' and continues down to the river (**A**). Here cross a road, turn left along the riverside path, joining the Wye Valley Walk, and follow it for nearly 1½ miles (2·5 km) through the steep-sided valley, which is thickly wooded on both sides.

Just before reaching Biblins suspension bridge, which was erected by the Forestry Commission, turn sharp left (**B**), almost immediately taking the right-hand path at a fork and following it steeply uphill. This next stage of the walk is fairly tortuous and you need to look out carefully for the indispensable yellow waymarks. On reaching a path junction turn right, continuing more gently uphill along a broad path and keeping by the boundary fence of Lady Park Wood National Nature Reserve on the right. Just after the path levels out turn sharp right, heading gently uphill again, and cross a track. Keep ahead, bear right at a fork, and at the next track turn left, almost immediately following a yellow arrow to the right. At the next fork bear right to reach the Near Hearkening Rock, a long mass of conglomerate rock and a superb viewpoint over the Wye Valley.

Continue downhill along a narrow, twisting path which passes below the overhanging rock, looking out for a yellow arrow where you turn right along another narrow, downhill path through some rather gloomy conifers to reach the Suck Stone. It has been claimed that this is the largest detached rock in the country and estimates of its weight vary from 4,000 to 14,000 tons. Continue past it, head downhill to a broad, stony track and turn left along it. Look out for a yellow arrow guiding you onto a narrow path, which bears left off the track and continues in an undulating manner through woodland to come out onto a road on the edge of the village of Staunton (**C**)

*At this point, those wishing to do the shorter version of the walk, omitting the fine viewpoint of the Buck Stone, can turn left along the road, rejoining the longer walk at (**E**) below.*

Cross the road, take the uphill tarmac lane almost opposite and turn right in front of a gate to continue along a narrow path. The path continues steadily uphill, keeping by a wall on the right most of the time, to reach

A walker in Highmeadow Woods

the Buck Stone (**D**), the highest point of the walk (915 feet (279 m)) and a magnificent viewpoint over the forest and Wye Valley with the Black Mountains on the horizon. This massive stone once rocked on its slender pedestal but was tipped over by vandals in 1885 and consequently smashed. It was later repaired and re-erected on its original site, but it no longer rocks.

From the Buck Stone continue along a track which curves to the left, giving more fine views over the Forest of Dean, and heads steadily downhill. Bear left on joining a tarmac lane, and where the lane bends to the right keep ahead along a narrow path which gently descends to rejoin the lane, cutting off a corner. Turn left and follow the lane downhill into Staunton, turning sharp right at a junction and then following the road as it curves left. Bear right at the next junction and continue through the village to the attractive, interesting cruciform church (**E**) which retains some of its original Norman arches and contains an unusual staircase leading to the pulpit. In the churchyard are the remains of an old cross.

Opposite the church and just before reaching the main road bear right along a track, and where the track bends sharply to the right keep ahead along a broad path, going gently uphill. Follow it as far as a junction of paths and turn left, looking out for a yellow arrow, soon bearing left again on joining a track. At a T-junction of tracks follow yellow arrows ahead along a narrow path which leads down to a road opposite the Long Stone (**F**). This, the last of the series of large rocks passed on the walk, is thought to have once been a meeting place for local tribes.

Cross the road, take the path to the left of the stone that keeps roughly parallel to the road, continue ahead on joining a track and bear left at a T-junction. On reaching a broader track bear slightly right, pass by the side of a forestry gate and keep ahead for a few yards to a junction of tracks. Here turn left, passing by another gate, and continue, taking the right-hand path at a fork and keeping by the edge of a campsite on the right.

Cross a tarmac road (**G**), take the track immediately ahead and follow it, more or less in a straight line, back to Symonds Yat. This is a lovely part of the walk — the track is fairly flat and well-surfaced and passes through delightful woodland above steep, thickly wooded slopes on the left. Finally it joins a broader track which leads directly to Yat Rock car park.

Useful organisations

The Countryside Commission,
John Dower House, Crescent Place,
Cheltenham, Gloucestershire GL50 3RA.
Tel: 0242 21381

The National Trust,
36 Queen Anne's Gate, London SW1H
9AS. Tel: 071 222 9251
(Severn Regional Office, Mythe End
House, Tewkesbury, Gloucestershire
GL20 6EB. Tel: 0684 850051
South Wales Regional Office,
The Kings Head, Bridge Street,
Llandeilo, Dyfed SA19 6BN.
Tel: 0558 822800)

Heart of England Tourist Board,
2 Trinity Street, Worcester WR1 2PW.
Tel: 0905 613132

Wales Tourist Board,
Brunel House, 2 Fitzalan Road, Cardiff
CF2 1UY. Tel: 0222 499909

The Ramblers' Association,
1/5 Wandsworth Road, London SW8
2LJ. Tel: 071 582 6878

The Forestry Commission,
Information Branch,
231 Corstorphine Road, Edinburgh EH12
7AT. Tel: 031 334 0303
(Local headquarters at Crown Offices,
Bank Street, Coleford, Gloucestershire
GL16 8BA. Tel: 0594 33057)

The Youth Hostels Association,
Trevelyan House, 8 St Stephen's Hill,
St Albans, Hertfordshire AL1 2DY.
Tel: 0727 55215

The Long Distance Walkers' Association,
Lodgefield Cottage, High Street,
Flimwell, Wadhurst, East Sussex TN5 7PH.
Tel: 058 087 341

The Council for the Protection of Rural
England,
4 Hobart Place, London SW1W 0HY.
Tel: 071 235 5959

The Council for the Protection of Rural
Wales,
Ty Gwyn, 31 High Street, Welshpool,
Powys SY21 7JP.
Tel: 0938 552525

Ordnance Survey,
Romsey Road, Maybush, Southampton
SO9 4DH.
Tel: 0703 792764/5 or 792749

Ordnance Survey maps of the Wye Valley and Forest of Dean

The Wye Valley and Forest of Dean area is covered by Ordnance Survey 1:50 000 scale (1¼ inches to 1 mile) Landranger map sheets 148, 149, 150, 161, 162 and 171. These all-purpose maps are packed with information to help you explore the area. Viewpoints, picnic sites, places of interest, caravan and camping sites are shown, as well as public rights of way information such as footpaths and bridleways.

To examine this area in more detail,
and especially if you are planning walks, Ordnance Survey Pathfinder maps at 1:25 000 (2½ inches to 1 mile) scale are ideal. Maps covering the area are:

1016 (SO 24/34)	1065 (SO 62/72)
1039 (SO 23/33)	1086 (SO 21/31)
1040 (SO 43/53)	1087 (SO 41/51)
1041 (SO 63/73)	1088 (SO 61/71)
1063 (SO 22/32)	1089 (SO 81/91)
1064 (SO 42/52)	

Also at the same scale are the Outdoor Leisure maps. Brecon Beacons – Eastern area number 13 and Wye Valley & Forest of Dean number 14 cover this area.

To get to the Wye Valley and Forest of Dean, use the Ordnance Survey Routemaster map number 7 Wales and the West Midlands at 1:250 000 (1 inch to 4 miles) scale.

Ordnance Survey maps and guides are available from most booksellers, stationers and newsagents.

Index